# SHUT UP, I'M TALKING!

---

## COMING OUT IN HOLLYWOOD
## AND MAKING IT TO THE MIDDLE

by

# JASON STUART

## WITH DAN DUFFY

CCB Publishing
British Columbia, Canada

Shut Up, I'm Talking!:
Coming Out in Hollywood and Making It to the Middle

Copyright ©2019 by Jason Stuart
ISBN-13    978-1-77143-393-8
First Edition

Library and Archives Canada Cataloguing in Publication
Title: Shut up, I'm talking! : coming out in Hollywood and making it to the middle
/ by Jason Stuart ; with Dan Duffy.
Names: Stuart, Jason, 1959- author.
Identifiers: Canadiana (print) 20190127031 | Canadiana (ebook) 20190127058 |
ISBN 9781771433938 (softcover) | ISBN 9781771433945 (PDF)
Subjects: LCSH: Stuart, Jason.
| LCSH: Motion picture actors and actresses—United States—Biography.
| LCSH: Gay motion picture actors and actresses—United States—Biography.
| LCSH: Television actors and actresses—United States—Biography.
| LCSH: Comedians—United States—Biography.
Classification: LCC PN2287.S78 A3 2019 | DDC 791.43092—dc23

Front cover artwork credit: Photo of Jason Stuart by Sean Black
Back cover artwork credit: Photo of Jason Stuart by Tilda Del Toro

Publisher:    CCB Publishing
              British Columbia, Canada
              www.ccbpublishing.com

For my mother, Gloria, who taught me how to survive, laugh, and how to get a man… but not necessarily keep him.

And who gave me the title of this book, by saying it to me countless times while growing up.

# Contents

# Acknowledgments

To Dan Duffy, for your willingness to write this book with me. All of your kindness and generosity is a gift. This book would not be done if it were not for you. I am forever grateful.

To Alexandra Paul, my real sister from another mother. For doing the "college girl" on all my work and making me look like I went to some sort of school. Also for your friendship and support through the hardest and best of times.

To Ernie Rhoads, my brother from another mother. And yes... so much funnier than me! The best friend a guy could have and a great travel buddy.

To Amanda, my touchstone whom I consider family. You have known me longer than any other person except my mother. Your willingness to keep showing up for me keeps me real.

To my sponsors in my twelve-step program friends: Michael Ferrera, Carolyn, Robin, Jason, and especially for my BFF David Hamilton and his sister Kim Bodell; for taking my calls and showing me that there is a higher power that will take care of me.

To Duncan Crabtree-Ireland, for mentoring me as a leader in the LGBTQ Community, and co-creating the SAG-AFTRA LGBTQ Committee with me. And to Ellen Hung and Adam Moore for their endless support of the SAG-AFTRA LGBTQ Committee which I continue to co-chair.

To Richard Weiss, without whom I would not have had a book deal. And to Carole Jordan, for taking the time to edit all the spelling, grammar, and the use of the same word over and over again!

To my comedian friends for your support over the years: Aida Rodriguez, Tiffany Haddish, Shang Forbes, Wendy Hammers, Jay Davis, Drew Carey, Damon Wayans, Helen Hong, Jennie McNulty, Vicki Barbolak, Adam Hunter, Randy Lubas, Brenda Petrakos, Beverly Berwald, Lexie Grace and Bob Perkell. You are my brothers and sisters in this world we call comedy. Thank you for the jobs and for giving me a family in stand-up. And most of all to Sheila Kay, for being the big sister I always needed and can always count on.

To all my actor friends for holding my hand and walking with me through our careers over and over again: Lydia Nicole, Dalila Ali Rajah, Paul Elia, Lee Garlington, Linna Carter, Danielle Moné Truitt, Scott Crawford, Joie Magidow, Jake Hunter, Daniyar, Terry Ray, Tilda Del Toro, Suze Hopper, Mitch Hara, Scott Krinsky and especially to Anna Garduna for teaching me to age gracefully. To my friend Jacquie Mendenhall, who was the first person who told me I was going to be a successful actor. And lastly to Alison Arngrim, for walking me through the whole process (with a lotta love) in writing this book.

To the filmmakers, acting coaches, producers, and casting people who changed me as an artist and gave me the confidence to move to the next level as an actor: Nate Parker, Sean Baker, Billy Clift, Darren Dean, Don Reo, Jimmy Valley, Dea Vise, Billy DaMota, Cathy Henderson, Bruce Cohen, Jackie Burch, Ivana Chubbuck, Larry Moss, Roy London, Nina Foch, Jim Lande, Chris Bergoch, Lisa Sanow, Keith Truesdell, Patrick Hasburgh, Stewart Wade, Mekhi Phifer, Daniel Ringey, James Widdoes, Ira Sachs, Terri Hanauer, and my pal Adam Belanoff.

To my agents and managers who stood behind me: Bonny Dore, Cathryn Jaymes, Daniel Ortega, Brenda P. Netzberger, Annie Schwartz, and most of all to my dear friend Shelly Weiss, for all of your love, support, friendship, and hard work for me for over twenty-five years.

To my dad, Lenny, and his wife Linda, who taught me to work hard and take care of myself. To my grandma, Molly, for giving me that extra squeeze of attention that I needed as a child. And especially to my mom, Gloria, who gave me a great sense of humor and loves me like no other.

And lastly to Barbra Streisand, who I don't know personally, but who gave a young gay Jewish boy hope at a very bleak time in his life, and showed him through her films and music that the world is full of possibilities.

# Foreword
## by Alexandra Paul

This is not going to be a witty, funny intro because I am rarely witty and funny - I will leave that to Jason. This is more of a love letter for one of my closest friends. A man whom I admire, love, and rely on for moral support and life advice. A friend with whom I am going to grow old. We are going to be two toothless actors, but we will still talk and talk and talk.

I met Jason in 1985 when I was the membership director of a non-profit I co-founded called Young Artists United. It was made up of young people in the entertainment industry who recognized the power of the media and wanted to give back. When Jason called me about joining, I still remember distinctly – over three decades later - sitting at the kitchen table talking to him, thoroughly enchanted with this outgoing, funny man on the other end of the line.

We met shortly thereafter at a YAU event, and bonded over saving the world. Then he saved me: for ten years, Jason was my sponsor as I overcame my eating disorder. We talked every day (no texting or emails back in the 1990s, so staying in touch meant speaking on the phone or in person), including when I was on location in faraway places like war torn Croatia. In the 1990s, an overseas call was extremely expensive, not to mention an overseas call from a hotel, so I would trudge in the winter cold to the nearby post office after a long day of filming to call Jason, hanging on for dear life to my Twelve Steps.

Even though he always brings his sense of humor, Jason also has a depth that he reveals only to a lucky few. I attribute that to the pain and adversity he has dealt with in his own life, and the grace with which he has overcome those challenges. With Jason, I can admit my darkest thoughts, my biggest fears, my least charitable feelings, and he will nod and accept me with all my flaws.

What probably most impresses me about Jason is his amazing work ethic and his ability to always think the best of people, even after the bullying and ostracism he experienced as a gay man. I remember being pissed off at someone whom I felt had not treated Jason with respect, and Jason said, "We don't know what is going on in people's lives when they act badly. They have stressful days, personal problems that seem overwhelming, and they lash out."

I told Jason he could be all Ghandi-like, but I was going be angry on his behalf anyway!

Jason has influenced me in so many positive ways since that day I first spoke with him on the phone in 1985. If you have not had the good luck to have him in your life for years and years like I have, the second best thing you can do is to get to know him from this book.

Learn from his experiences, be inspired by his moral courage, and laugh at his jokes. You'll be glad you did.

# Prologue

## Simply Barbra

The poster was a cartoon of her wearing roller-skates, and she was upside-down… funny, huh? The marquee was yellow with black letters. She had only two "a's" in her name. Strangely powerful and original. I was drawn to it, partially by its peculiarity (to which I could relate). It's as if she was saying to the world, "Keep your third 'a.' I don't really need it."

Barbra.

I'd heard the name before from the gal who owned this little store called Sadie, where I worked. Apparently she was a big deal, big enough that my grandmother Klara knew of her. She was so keen to see Barbra's new film *Hello, Dolly!* that she was adamant my dad buy the whole family tickets a week before the showing, a practice commonplace today but not even whispered about in the late 1960's.

My knowledge of Ms. Streisand was limited at best. I couldn't tell you if *Hello, Dolly!* was her second film or her twenty-second film. I'd heard she was from Brooklyn and that her dialect sounded like some of the people I grew up with. People would sometimes talk about her acting or singing, and that it was something to behold.

But personally, that was the limit of my knowledge base. I hadn't even realized at the time that she only commandeered two a's for her first name, until I stood in front of the marquee that day.

I just had to see her.

I had ridden my green Schwinn Stingray with the banana seat by the Pan Pacific Theatre on Beverly Boulevard, a place where movies received a second life long after their initial run. I wanted to see what was playing and look at the movie posters to find out what was coming up, which was the 1960's version of Siskel and Ebert.

I loved movies so much as a child. My mother used to drop us at the theatre for a double feature so she could go shopping or do… whatever she did. My brother Steve and I would watch the first showing of the day. Sometimes, we watched the film twice or three times while waiting for her to pick us up. Thankfully, the ushers didn't care if we stayed to watch the same film over and over again.

Each time a movie started, I would pick a character and go through all of his or her emotions as they were acted out on the screen… a habit that would serve me well later in life as an actor. My brother, on the other hand, crawled around on the floor while reenacting scenes from some of the action films like *The Great Escape* to break up his boredom of daily viewing number three. I would always join in.

When my mother came back for us, we'd beg and plead and wheel and deal to get her to stay for one more film. She would agree if the movie was really good. It was such a wonderful escape from the reality of a world that would only become more confusing as I grew older.

If there was one thing that I loved as much as the movies, it was riding my bike. Many times, I'd ride around town with my friends without a care in the world. But on this day… like most days… it was just me and my olive Stingray with the banana seat. That bike was my freedom, much like a teenager's first beater of a car when he turns sixteen. In fact, I probably would have kept riding that day had the name on that marquee not somehow stopped time.

Barbra Streisand in *Funny Girl*.

'Wow, that's the same actress my grandma bought tickets in advance to see *Hello, Dolly!* I thought. 'Maybe I'll stop in to see it so that when I go to the movies with my family next week, I'll be caught up on her.'

So I parked my bike, paid my money, and found my seat. As the screen came to life, I was not prepared for what was about to happen.

The first notes of the overture to *Funny Girl* began to swell, eliciting the faintest hint of a stir in my soul. I didn't know how or why, but I felt something big, something life altering, was about to happen.

And then there was the walk. The fur. The pause. The visage. As she looked into a mirror and said with a self-deprecating tone, "Hello, gorgeous," that was it. Just two words in, I was in love, hooked, and a true fan.

And there I was, sweet as pie, tough as leather, belting out those same lyrics about how I was the greatest star by far, but no one knew it.

Oh. My. God.

As the dichotomy of Fanny Brice erupted from the screen like a Palm Springs Desert after a storm, I knew exactly who this woman was: she was me.

I was drawn to her power to be different, and her essence echoed my own: funny on the outside, yet sad on the inside. It was my first glimpse into the truth that so many of us use comedy to protect us from our true selves.

But she wasn't hiding from her pain. She embraced it.

And she was Jewish!

And that voice!

And funny!

And yes… a woman!

Oy!

But I'm a boy? How's this gonna work out for me? How do I fit into this world?

Barbra was the biggest female "everything" star in the world from the late 60's to the early 90's. In the movies, it was her, Jane Fonda, and then everyone else… no one could touch her success, and she was so unapologetic about it all which made me love her even more.

But even if you take away her film career, no one has ever had that voice. Without Barbra there would be no Lady Gaga, no Beyoncé, no Madonna, no Cher, nor even Bette Midler. Ever. She is, was, and will always be… it.

She stood out, even in a golden age of acting for men, as well. Dustin Hoffman (who to this day is my favorite actor) and the dynamic Al Pacino were the male stars I gravitated to, already showing why they were perhaps two of the most important actors in the history of cinema.

But Barbra held a certain special place in my heart and soul, which I have to say made things almost strangely awkward. What was even more bizarre to me was that if I was attracted to Omar Sharif (Nick Arnstein, Fanny Brice's husband in *Funny Girl*), who was I left to be but Barbra?

As I walked out of the theatre that day, I found myself relating to someone I didn't even know in that very rare way that only happens a few moments in a lifetime. I saw myself in her, and it only confused me more.

I was a boy, and the idea of identifying so strongly with a woman while going through my own private hell known as puberty confused me to no end. And as my junior high hormones started to engage and rage, I identified even more with her… as in a choice of crushes and attraction. In other words…

… it was not the girls who held my gaze. It was the boys.

Oh no.

But at least, I was no longer alone. I had Barbra.

# SHUT UP, I'M TALKING!

# 1

## Gotta Move; Gotta Get Out

It was October of 1941. The Nazis had been running roughshod throughout Europe for the better part of two years, and they took particular delight in making life in Poland miserable, including a town in the far south of the country called Stanisławów, to be known as Stanislaus for the rest of this book.

Armageddon was coming.

Decades prior in 1906, a baby boy named Jack Greif was born. A baby girl named Klara Tishler was born in 1909. As they were each born into a family of no less than ten children, both Klara and Jack's parents were quite busy during those years.

Those poor, poor women. Pregnant for years on end. How did they do it? And they weren't even Catholic.

Oy!

These two bundles of joy would eventually meet, get married, and bring a bundle of joy of their own into the world in 1931, a son they named Leonard, whom they would affectionately call Lenny. Seven years later, Lenny's brother Mike was born… just as things were hitting the proverbial fan in Eastern Europe.

Before the invasion of Poland, the Greif family lived quite well. In Yiddish terms, Jack was a macher, a person of influence who gets things done. He was the manager of a large steel company and also owned and ran a grocery store. He was a hard worker, a practice that was instilled into his children.

They had a house in the same town as all of their brothers and sisters, and they were a tight-knit community. They lived together, worked together, and raised each other's children. Together.

They got their gossip, their stories, their rumors, and their news from the grapevine, or the 1940's Polish version of CNN… with a little TMZ for flavor. The story coming through in early October of 1941 was news that no one wanted to hear… or believe.

The Nazis were marching towards Stanislaus, arresting everyone they saw as unfit along the way. Gays. Gypsies.

And Jews.

Now Klara was rumored to be clairvoyant, bossy… or as Jews call it, a yenta. When she heard the news, she knew that this was no idle gossip. Without a breath or a pause, she said to Jack, "We must leave. I feel it in my bones that something bad is coming."

Can you imagine having to get up, pack what you can carry, and get on a train with your spouse and your children with absolutely no idea where you're going, or what you're going to do when you get to wherever you're going? Yet this is what she was proposing with those first three words.

We. Must. Leave.

Now like in any good game of telephone, the final story you hear is usually nothing like the original broadcast, and everyone thought that Klara was out of her mind for making that choice. But her intuition was unshakeable, and her decision was final.

Jack said, "I'm going to be a target if I get up and leave. I run a factory, and people know that I'm being watched closely. I will quietly go and settle our affairs at the bank and close up the house. I will meet you in a few days."

And this would all have to be done without the benefit of any sort of direct communication. No Internet, no cell phone, no social media…

nothing but their voices.

Klara agreed. It made sense to be as careful as you could be in a situation bordering on utter chaos or even death. They had picked a place to rendezvous, and the plan was set in motion. They would go to the station, blend in with all the other soon-to-be refugees, and wait a day or more for the slim chance of surviving by getting on a train for God-knows-where.

Jack would make sure his family boarded safely before taking care of the other arrangements, only to repeat the process himself a few days later. It might work. It could work. It had to work.

And it would work... only not how Jack had envisioned.

The tension was thick in Stanislaus, now part of present-day Ukraine. As he promised, Jack started to tie up his loose ends while Klara and her two boys walked to the train station... eleven-year-old Lenny carrying four-year-old Mike on his shoulders. They arrived at their destination and waited.

Taking a break from his own work and wanting to make sure things were going to plan, Jack arrived at the station to see them safely on board once they got the chance. As they stood there waiting, he and Klara went over their plan to make sure they both had it straight.

After what seemed like an eternity waiting in line for their turn, it was finally time for the family to get on the train. The boys boarded, and Klara stayed near the entrance of the train car for one last sweet kiss goodbye.

Only, there would be no goodbye.

As the train started to pull away, Klara wrapped her arms around Jack for one last kiss and pulled him on board with every ounce of strength she could muster.

Surprise.

All the plans, all the loose ends, all the future steps were thrown out... now just a memory on a train platform in Stanislaus.

Their unplanned future lived in their two young sons, and their two suitcases that held every stitch of clothing and the few photographs they had with them. They went from having everything to almost nothing in the blink of an eye.

But in her heart, Klara knew she did the right thing. She could not explain it, but she knew what was to come, and the fear of what she saw in her mind's eye, as the legend goes, her hair turned white that very night.

Two days later, on October 12 of 1941, news came in from the grapevine. Bloody Sunday. Over ten thousand Jews were shot dead by the SS and buried in hastily dug mass graves. Everyone in the town had been murdered. Brothers. Sisters. Aunts. Uncles. Cousins. Parents.

Everyone.

Call it God, call it clairvoyance, call it outrageous fortune or blind luck, but Klara knew it was coming. In fact, throughout the rest of the war, she had an uncanny knack of when it was time to move. Much like the film *The Pianist* with the unforgettable Oscar-winning performance by Adrien Brody, Jack and Klara and their two sons moved from place to place, from the ghetto to the countryside and back again, always a step ahead of those trying to kill them.

They were on the run for four long years. They slept in farms, ghettos, and hidden places in kind people's homes… even under the floorboards like in the film *Inglourious Basterds*. They were literally risking their lives every day.

They were only able to stop running as the liberation finally came. The Greif family ended up finding refuge in the German/American displaced persons camp called Ansbach, governed by the good ol' United States army.

I just love a man in uniform!

After they settled in Ansbach, they applied to emigrate with the rest of the poor, tired, and huddled masses. The process would take another four years, but the hopes and dreams of one day eventually making it to the United States was worth the wait for Jack and Klara. Even Lenny was excited at the prospect of his new life. He fancied himself as a living Wikipedia.

"I can't wait to tell the Americans just how bad it was for us, and what we had to do to survive," he would say to anyone who listened.

It was only later that he realized what he and his family had been through was nothing compared to what went on in the concentration camps. They had heard the rumors, but they had no idea of the pure horror that actually existed until they made a safe passage to America.

But the wait was maddening. The conditions at Ansbach were not of the Four Seasons variety. No air conditioning in the summer. No central heat in the winter. They ate what was put in front of them, and they were not allowed to leave. Lenny would later describe it as a place where you felt trapped and claustrophobic.

It reminds me of conditions that many refugees and immigrants face today trying to come into this country. It makes me sad that we haven't made much progress since 1945.

That improbable emigration would only happen thanks to a family in the United States who agreed to sponsor the Polish refugees. They were the aunt and uncle of one of Jack and Klara's parents, and they were only too happy to help their family members forge a new future.

Their names were also Jack and Klara, and they would be forever known as The Aunt and The Uncle to our family. Just knowing that some members of their family survived and left mostly intact made their hearts sing, as they had lost so many to these unspeakable atrocities.

I was lucky enough have The Aunt attend my bar mitzvah. Apparently her hearing didn't work too well. While I was just trying to get through my big reading (completely botching it due to my incompetence at Hebrew School), she kept yelling, "Who's gonna cut the chicken?!"

And this was her inside voice. The Aunt was apparently hard of hearing in her later years, but she saved our lives, so she gets a pass. It was thanks to her and The Uncle that Jack, Klara, Lenny, and Mike Greif arrived in New York City on March 17, 1949. It was a fitting symbol of what this family endured to get to the new world… a battle to hold your own in a world that is not always kind.

They changed, and really saved, the lives of a lineage. They will always be considered a gift from God. As the son of Lenny Greif, I'm eternally grateful to everyone who made their impossible journey... possible.

# 2

## This Is Us

New York City was a tough place for some in the 1950's. It was even tougher if you did not know the language. Lenny and his family had only been in the United States for five years, a Polish refugee of the Holocaust, with a detour in Ansbach, a German/American refugee camp.

Their accents were thick and their syntax was poor. Once while his younger brother was applying for a job, Mike walked into the office and said in his thick Polish accent, "I'm here for job."

Unimpressed, the receptionist said, "Take a chair and we'll be right with you."

So Mike picked up the chair, walked out of the building, and brought it home on the subway.

Seriously.

It was a tough time for Lenny and his family. They didn't have the tools to adjust well to American life, at least at first. They had little to no support by way of therapy. They did not have the coping skills to deal with the PTSD of constantly running from the Nazis. Lenny's parents were learning their adoptive new-native tongue via television.

To the moon, Alice! From *The Honeymooners*.

Lucy, what have you done this time? From *I Love Lucy*.

Still, they had a survivalist instinct, and they would make it... regardless of their linguistic shortcomings. Lenny was charming and witty when he had to be, and he was a hard worker. He was handsome, and he had more than his fair share of dates with the opposite sex...

... including a fateful night in 1955.

The setting was a nightclub in Forest Hills, Long Island, where the legendary singer Don Cornell was performing. Lenny looked good that night, hair combed, clothes pressed, single and ready to mingle. He was to meet up with Eleanor, his half of the double-date for the evening.

A sultry brunette, Eleanor was quite the catch. Her parents owned an old-time soda fountain, the type of place that sold hot fudge sundaes and candy and cigarettes. They would make a fine match for a night on the town.

Fate, the stars, and primal magnetism had other ideas.

The women arrived, and there she was. Gloria... a vision like he had never seen. She was blonde, beautiful, tough, sexy... a real Brooklyn girl. Picture Marilyn Monroe... only Jewish. She had a look that could melt a man's heart, a voice that could raise his blood pressure, and a set of curves that could stop him dead in his tracks.

She was to be the date of his friend, which meant he had his work cut out for him. Gloria bewitched him before she even said hello, which I'm sure did not go over well with Eleanor, her best friend.

And truth be told, the man Gloria was with that night was not even her boyfriend. Her actual boyfriend at that time was a young man named Arthur who was the only one she was crazy about. He was a Jewish Robert De Niro. The trouble with Arthur was that he was out of town a lot on business.

As Gloria once said, "He was a hustler, a bad boy. He was always doing this or doing that, and I only saw him when he wanted too. But our chemistry was undeniable."

And he was out of town on that particular Saturday night, leaving her dateless as usual... which was ridiculous when you were as gorgeous as Gloria. When another man asked her out for the evening, it was not so much, "I'd love to," as it was, "I've got nothing better to do."

She had her own thoughts of who ran the show, which was quite the feat in the 1950's. She was strong, smart, assertive, and she would kowtow to no one. Lenny simply had no idea of what he was about to get into.

Of course, neither did Gloria.

At their first meeting, he was captivated. She… whatever.

Gloria thought, 'Ah… he's alright,' which would be a bit of an early definer in their relationship. She was not one to sleep around, but she was also not a wallflower. Truth be told, she was still a virgin. She dated a few men at any given time, refusing to go steady with any of them. She was waiting for Arthur to come back to town to claim her.

Like many women at the time, Gloria's mother, Molly, put the fear of God into her about the evils of sexuality. Gloria explained: "For God's sake, my mother said if I even kissed a guy, I'd end up pregnant. And besides, I was too young for that."

She was too young for a lot of things that she ended up doing anyway. One night, she and Lenny went to New Jersey to a place called The Flagship. Then they went to Minsky's Burlesque, which had been illegal since April of 1937, driven underground by the laws of decency at the time. Then it was dancing the Rhumba to *Papa Loves Mambo*, followed by way too many drinks.

It could have been lust, like, the excitement of breaking the rules, or simply too much booze. Maybe it was the laughs, or the rebellion of being out on the town away from her crazy relationship with her parents. Maybe it was a combination of all of it. Regardless, Lenny and Gloria consummated… something… that night. He was twenty-two. She was seventeen.

Things were changing for Gloria. And soon, they would change even more as she would shortly have a new title: Teen Mom; the Jewish Years. Gloria was pregnant. Many words described her reaction. Fearful. Shocked. Helpless. The most appropriate: alone.

Gloria did not know Lenny well. She didn't even know where he worked. After telling her mother the dreaded news that no mother wanted to hear in 1955, she asked Molly for help in finding my dad. She tried to reach out to Lenny and his family by phone on several occasions to no avail.

Undeterred, Molly went to the home of Jack and Klara, Lenny's parents, and in no uncertain terms told them that either Lenny would marry her daughter, or she would take him to court. Gloria was just below New York's age of consent at the time. There were laws.

Jack and Klara didn't quite come off as sympathetic. They barely spoke English, and they had no idea who my mom was. Was this crazy American girl trying to trap their son, or was she simply a girl in trouble?

And they were not being presented with an easy choice. It would be the aisle, or the courtroom. There was no door number three in this episode of *Let's Make a Deal.* Only rich kids could disappear, which was not an option for Gloria... the daughter of a salesman who sold perfume and neckties out of the trunk of his car.

They said they would get back to her, but they weren't about to do so. Like the ostrich, they figured that if they couldn't see it, it wasn't there. Problem solved. However, if Jack and Klara thought ignoring the situation would be the end of it, they had no idea of the determination of Brooklyn Jews. They eat "cold shoulder" for breakfast. And they like it.

Molly would not back down... not when the fate of her daughter was at stake.

At first, Lenny refused to believe what had happened. Then, he refused to acknowledge his responsibility. But Molly persisted. Because Gloria was not of legal age in the state of New York, he had the very real possibility of being found guilty of statutory rape. He relented by saying that he would marry her, with the proviso that there be a blood test determining that the child was his.

In my father's defense, he told me he always loved my mother, and that he wanted to be with her from the first time he saw her. But this would mean his dreams of being a photographer, along with all the trappings that come from being a free agent in America, would have to be put on hold… possibly permanently… to raise a family. He had to be sure.

With the promise of impending nuptials in place, Lenny's family said that they would get back to Molly with final details. Only, they had no intention of doing so. These European Jews had lived through far worse than anything a few Brooklyn Jews could throw at them. Or so they thought.

The Europeans grossly underestimated the resolve of their Brooklyn counterparts: Molly was no one to be messed with. Born in Boston in 1908 to Russian immigrants, she had lived through more than her fair share of anguish. She lost a four-year-old brother who was hit by a car. As a result, her mother, Sarah, dissolved into a state of unaffectionate madness.

It was said her mother would never leave the house, and was prone to moments of utter senselessness, occasionally wearing three dresses at the same time. Sometimes, instead of letting her daughters come inside to eat a meal, she would lower food down in a basket tied to a rope from the window of their third floor walk-up to the street.

Sarah's chronic detachment was, sadly, commonplace. Once when she was nineteen, Molly went on a bicycle ride to Canada with some of her girlfriends. When she got back a few weeks later, no one had even acknowledged that she had been gone.

Molly was utterly abandoned by her mother; she was not about to let her daughter suffer the same fate. She would stand beside Gloria to fight for her every step of the way, and fight she did.

A showdown loomed, and it would be settled by the New York justice system. Molly and Gloria arrived at the courthouse. If things weren't scary enough for the young mother-to-be, the two attorneys that Lenny brought with him almost pushed her over the edge. Molly found the whole situation odd.

'How would he know to hire attorneys?' she thought. Maybe a co-worker suggested it, maybe a relative; no one really knows, but they frightened the life out of Gloria.

"They were fat… these huge men with big beer bellies were terrifying. I'll never forget it," Gloria recalled decades later. They made a terrifying lifelong impression on her.

While intimidating to the women, the attorneys made absolutely no difference to the African American judge… who was a rarity in 1955.

And they turned out to be worthless to Lenny, as well, as the judge handed down his ruling: because Gloria was under the age of consent at the time of conception, Lenny would be on the hook for statutory rape. He could either marry Gloria, or get to know his new neighbors in the New York Penitentiary.

Here comes the bride…

Without so much as a proposal, two weeks later in a wedding hall somewhere in East Manhattan, on April 3rd of 1955, Lenny and Gloria were married. To this day, for what is normally one of the happiest memories of a woman's life, my mom does not remember the exact location of the ceremony. All she knows is that she gave him her virginity, his freedom from jail, and a son seven months after her vows.

His name would be Steven.

Looking back, I think my mom got her strength to go through with the marriage from her own mom, Molly. Even through the sometimes difficult moments their relationship revealed, my mom always had a special place in her heart for Molly.

And Molly had a lot of special things in her apartment that were not actually hers. Apparently, Molly was a kleptomaniac. When my mom was little, she saw a bathing suit on a clothesline that she liked and remarked about it to Molly. The next day, that same bathing suit showed up!

What are the chances?

But that was Molly… a special force of nature in the world.

I never knew the story of how my parents got married until I was well into my late teens. I was in an acting class and the subject of early birth came up. I said my brother was born early at seven months because my mom had fallen in the shower. All the actors laughed, and my friend Jacquie Mendenhall told me that it was an old wives' tale. Apparently a lot of people fell in the shower in the 1950s.

I laugh when people say that life was simpler back then. It wasn't. At all.

# 3

# Stuart Little

I was born at Westchester Hospital in the Bronx on January 13, 1959, at 1:47am. At seven pounds-eight ounces, I wasn't slim. My mother was 21... an age when people are still trying to lose their own puppy fat... let alone having a child, especially one the girth of a decent sized watermelon.

And I was her second-born... a save the marriage child, as the tale was told to me.

Oh. The irony.

They named me Stuart Ted Greif, and from all accounts I was a normal happy baby for my first three months of life, which is about the time that the honeymoon period ceased.

No one is quite sure how or why, but I somehow lost the vast majority of the water in my system. Think dehydration on speed. My mom, who was not quite prepared for my medical predicament, called my dad at work in a panic.

"Lenny, what do I do? Stuart seems really sick," she said.

These were the days when you couldn't just drop everything for a sick child. "Wait until I get off work," he said. "I can't leave right now. When I'm done, we'll take the baby to the doctor."

Apparently that was not the answer my mother was looking for, especially when I turned purple. Freaked out beyond imagination, she called the one person she knew would give it to her straight.

Molly. Her mom. One of the first loves of my own life.

"Mom, what do I do? He's purple!"

Molly did not bat an eyelid. "You take that kid to the hospital. You get in a cab and you take him to the hospital now!" Molly said.

Excuse me? What was that last part? Get into a cab? Was she serious?

In those days, my grandmother would have needed to save Elizabeth Taylor, herself, to warrant the cost of a cab. It was unheard of, especially when you simply took the subway everywhere. Why would you waste so much money on a cab? But my mother took her advice. She carried me into the cab and the driver rushed us to the hospital.

When we arrived, my condition was serious to the point that they had to perform hypodermoclysis, a ridiculously hard way of saying that they needed to insert an IV tube into my leg and have fluids dripped into my body so that my skin could absorb and redistribute them throughout my system. My mom says, "I had to have my blood changed."

I was very close to dying. My grandmother was so frightened that when she was at the hospital, she saw some nuns in the hallway and spontaneously turned Catholic. This Jewish woman asked them to pray for her grandbaby, and they were only too happy to oblige.

This is who Molly was. She did what had to be done, no matter the circumstance, no matter what anybody thought.

However, the conversion to Christ was only temporary. Her hypocrisy only went so far.

My father went to the hospital after work, having absolutely no idea just how serious the situation was until his arrival. He was so overcome with grief that he ran into the bathroom and wept.

Like most men, my dad always wanted to be the one who fixed things. He wanted to control the situation, to handle all things that need handling, and to be the one to make everything right. This was one of the things he couldn't control.

Thanks to 1959 modern medicine, I survived, and from everything

I've been told, thrived... much to the chagrin of my brother. He was older, and not the center of my parents' universe after my birth, so he picked his shots and tortured me with all manner of objects at his disposal. Once, my mother took both of us out in the snow. I know I was young, but I have the recollection of my brother throwing snowballs at me while I sat defenseless in my stroller.

He was an angry kid for most of my childhood. I was his punching bag. Let's just say that even to this day, I have never been his favorite person.

My mother should have known better... she and snow didn't mix very well. Two years after my parents got married, Gloria lost her wedding ring in the snow and was unable to find it. When she told my father, she quipped, "So does this mean that our marriage is over?"

I don't believe he thought it was as funny at the time as she did. Knowing her, she may or may not have been joking.

Needless to say, I don't make it a habit of being anywhere near snow. It's one of the many reasons I call Los Angeles home. And I would not be in Los Angeles if it was not for my father. He was a tie cutter, a skill he picked up and ran with like nobody's business.

Nowadays, I can't think of anything that isn't created by an automated process. But back then, Lenny Greif became so good, so fast, and so adept at cutting ties, a company headhunted him from New York to Los Angeles to do so on the west coast.

He created a method that made him in demand.

"Always make yourself indispensable," he would tell me.

And they were going to pay him a lot more money than he was already making to do it. So he accepted the offer after consulting with his parents, but before consulting with Gloria. And California here we come!

Swimming pools! Movie stars!

My mother was quite perturbed. For starters, she has never, ever been a fan of change, and this had change plastered all over it. It would mean a new life to lead, a new home to make, and an entirely different set of sensibilities. The ethos of everything being built on brick and mortar and sweat and tears and everything that made New York, New York, was not... Los Angeles. We might as well have been moving to a foreign country.

But the fear of losing her way of life and routines was not what my mom was the most scared about. She dreaded saying goodbye to everyone she knew and loved, especially Molly, her mother, her bedrock, her support system.

And in reality, had I been older and known exactly what we were getting into, I would have been nervous, too. Molly was my own surrogate mother. She was smitten with me from the moment I was born. I was smitten with her from the moment I knew what smitten actually meant. She took the time to listen to me. She saw me, she heard me... which is something I still seem to be looking for in a man.

The move was only the latest in a line of major disappointments for Gloria. She didn't ask for the complicated relationship she had with her parents. She didn't expect to end up with anyone but Arthur. She never had any intention of becoming a mother at eighteen. And she never planned on moving out of New York.

She was young and flamboyant, and truth be told, deeply unhappy with my dad. She knew she made a terrible mistake, and she felt that she was unable to become the woman she hoped she was going to be... whoever that was.

Of course, Lenny was no happier, battling PTSD from running almost his entire childhood from the Nazis during World War II, hiding between the ghettos and the countryside during the Holocaust. And his life had been such a whirlwind since arriving in America. The fast-paced life of New York City probably didn't do him any favors. Maybe he saw this as a way to slow the madness that seemed to constantly surround him.

Of course, he would also be saying goodbye to his own support network, including his mother and father, Jack and Klara. This move would not be easy on any of them. But the lure of money and a new beginning beckoned from the west coast. So my father loaded up the family into his 1953 green Chevrolet with a yellow top. He drove while my terrified mother rode shotgun. My brother and I camped out in the back seat... he being three-and-a-half, me being all of nine months. When my mother needed to separate us, she simply held me on her lap in the front seat. No one wore a seat belt. That's the way we did it in those days.

Three thousand miles-plus in that car did not do a whole lot for our family bonding time. My brother... a constant troublemaker... spent a good two thousand of those miles throwing things out of the window. At one point, he threw out a bunch of baby food jars onto the freeway, causing a flat tire to a motorist behind us. It did wonders for my mom's mood.

Soon after arriving, my dad's first job didn't work out. Instead of letting it defeat him, he found an even better job.

And then everything changed in what is one of the most indescribable sequences in my entire life. Call it missing our brood, call it the lure of palm trees and warm sunshine, call it saying goodbye to those brutal New York winters, but almost every single member of my family followed us out to Los Angeles.

And when I say followed, I mean really followed. My whole family ended up living in the same block of apartment buildings on Guthrie Avenue.

It all started just a single year after we moved to California. My dad's parents, Jack and Klara, were the first to arrive in 1960. They were followed in 1961 by Molly and Bob, my mom's parents, who ended up buying a four-plex where we eventually moved... living right across from them on the top floor. The closeness that Molly and I shared would continue. I was over the moon.

More relatives would soon follow. My great-uncle Dave moved across the street with his wife, Millie. Millie was older than Dave, and... well... she wasn't Jewish. Dave might as well have stuck an ice pick in my grandfather's eye while simultaneously kicking him in the groin with the sole of an old golf shoe. It would have hurt a lot less than him marrying a gentile. Quite the scandal at the time.

My uncle Mike and his wife Leona were the last to arrive, complete with my cousin Mitch in tow. He's six weeks younger than me, something he never lets me forget.

By the time the migration was complete, it felt like an entire Jewish neighborhood was transplanted from one coast to another. Except for Millie. But we won't talk about Millie. The family only talked about her under their breath.

A lot.

By today's standards, the thought of that much family living in such close proximity to each other is like a bad episode of *Dr. Phil*. Yet that's how it was back then. Family was everything, and for better or worse, we had each other. We were on top of each other, in each other's business, talked and gossiped about each other, and most of all... loved each other.

We had our own insulated familial commune. We were, for lack of a better word, cloistered.

Like nuns.

But Jewish.

And louder.

Oy!

# 4

## It Was the Worst of Times,
## It Was the Worst of Times

My Dad was a classic example of America being the land of opportunity. He went from immigrant, to janitor, to young husband and father, to revolutionary tie cutter in the space of just a few years. It was his innovation as a businessman that brought us to the west coast.

So true to my father's form in life of moving two steps forward and a step and a half back, his first job in "the schmatta (or rag) business" didn't work out. Yet he would not be discouraged. A company named Castle Neckwear was keen to meet the man from Europe with the secret skills to cut neckties in half the time, so they hired him.

Castle Neckwear was owned by Don Stark and Dick Baron. One had the same exact birthday as my mom, while the other had the same exact birthday as my dad. They brought him in, and he started cutting ties.

But Lenny Greif had bigger plans.

Over the course of thirty-five years, he went from tie cutter, to assistant manager, to manager, to vice president, and eventually part-owner. Yet he was not satisfied with the success he had already achieved. He wanted more. For his next endeavor, he went from part-owner of Castle Neckwear to local real estate mogul without skipping a beat. It seemed like everything he touched, business wise, turned to gold.

Throughout my own career, I've often emulated his work ethic. We've both been regarded as hard workers in our chosen craft. Of course, success in business is built over time; Hollywood is a different animal, where hard work is often overshadowed by the right-place-right-time overnight-success story. In other words, a star is born, not a star is made.

We'll get to that later.

Financially, he did very, very well for his family, and I'm glad that he was so successful. Because while his work life was the American dream, his home life was the American Horror Story. And why? Because he was married to a woman who would never be capable of being in love with him.

From the time I can remember, there was the screaming, the arguing, and the yelling from two people with not a single care about the response that was coming. Neither listened to a word the other said, and both resented not feeling seen or heard. They were just not suited for each other in this world.

Yet I was completely ignorant that anything was wrong because I really didn't know any better.

Isn't this how everyone acted? Didn't every mom run down the street screaming in cha-cha heels, a push up bra, and a hair-piece that reached to the sky?

Their script was etched in stone at this point. They'd fight, she'd walk out the door, get in the car, drive around the block a couple of times, come back, park the car, get out, and walk across the porch to her parents' house.

She would seek them out all the time because, in reality, they were the only people she had. They were her safe space, panic room, and shrink all at once. I say "shrink" because no one could spell psychotherapy back then, let alone define it.

With them, she could rest and be heard and fit in. She desperately wanted their approval because she loved them... and because they were just about the only adults who would listen to her.

Not too many people got her, and they certainly didn't know what to think of her. I'm not even sure my father approved of her after their first date, a feeling shared among every other woman within five square miles once they thought they got to know her.

The other moms in the neighborhood were wary of her womanly wiles. She was an insanely flirtatious woman... young, sexy, and needing a lot of attention. She certainly wasn't getting it from my dad.

And oh, did these women take notice; it was hard not to. My mom looked like the love child of Marilyn Monroe and Barbra Streisand, with Danny Kaye as my father!

I remember sitting on the stoop one day, playing with my friends, while a gaggle of the neighborhood moms kibitzed about where to get their prescription drugs filled. There was no need for drug dealers in those days. With one simple check-in with the grapevine, my mom knew where to get the pills she needed.

When she came outside to hang with the wives, I overheard one of the women say, "Watch out, here comes Gloria. Hang on to your husbands."

It should have bothered me when they said things about my mom, but it didn't. She wasn't the most trusted girl on the block, but she was popular with everyone... even with the women who secretly reviled her at times.

And she was so funny!

I adored her, and she adored me. I was her unabashed favorite. I know you're not supposed to say that, but I think it happens to many kids and parents; somehow, your souls just click and that becomes the course of your relationship.

Of course, with a brother like mine, I could have been an axe murderer and still would have been the favorite. I was the center of her universe... when she was able to make me that center, which was not nearly as often as I would have liked.

I'm pretty certain my brother knew his place in the pecking order and resented it. He was born too soon to a teenage mom who didn't know what to do with a kid, and a young father who seemed to need his parents more than anyone living under his own roof.

She and my father were obsessed with their bad marriage. And the cheating. And the lying. And the acting out. And the everything that went on between the European Jews and the Brooklyn Jews. I swear, Catholics and atheists have more in common. It was like we were from different lifestyles, countries, and worlds.

Oh wait... we were!

And nobody switched sides. There was no double dipping, no secret agent dealings like in the movies. If my mom had a problem, she would never in a million years seek the council of my dad's folks, and vice versa. Everyone had to take a side and defend it 'til the end.

My siblings are still holding on to all that pain fifty years later.

Me? I was afraid of almost everyone in my family. Oh sure, I loved them... to a point, but I always kept a relatively safe distance. However, I was obsessed with my mom's mom... my grandmother, Molly. She always had a minute and a half for me, no matter how busy she was.

A kind word. A squeeze. A kiss. A crust-less peanut butter and jelly sandwich after school.

There is nothing quite so fulfilling in life than the simplicity of being loved. With Molly's affection and my mother's adoration, coupled with them treating me like I was the smartest and bestest child in the history of children, I really did feel like the world revolved around me.

And then... my sister, Karen, was born.

Oy!

Don't get me wrong, I wanted a sister. At least... I thought I wanted a sister.

But I learned rather quickly that I was not going to have quite the fuss made of me like I was used to, especially from my mom. She wanted the dress-up baby girl with all the ribbons and bows that did not come with having boys.

Thankfully, I didn't have long to dwell on it. I had school to start.

I remember my first day of kindergarten like it was yesterday. I was absolutely, positively, over-the-moon to go to school. I couldn't wait to meet all the new kids, play with the new toys, and learn the new things.

My mom brought my sister with us to drop me off as she was still just a baby at the time. No sooner did we get there when some kid hit my sister with a building block by accident, and she started to wail. You would think the kid had been just shy of being decapitated by my mother's reaction. It was now abundantly clear that my big day was no longer my day. It was all about the baby girl. It was now her day.

Oh, and can we say "daddy's girl?"

The game was over, and I lost.

Karen – in, Stuart – out.

However, apart from the first half of day one, I loved kindergarten. The year was broken up into two parts, K-A and K-B. My first teacher was Mrs. Cable. She had this blonde bouffant hairdo, big perky breasts, and was in every way a knockout. All the dads would fake being sick at work so they could come to pick up their kids from school, a clever ruse to get a glimpse of her legs, her miniskirt, and her huge... bouffant hairdo.

Well that's what I would have looked at. It was a very popular style at the time!

The second half of the year, K-B, was Mrs. Shane. All I remember is taking off my shoes and sliding around on the wooden floors in my socks. I loved it. It's pretty nice when your only memory of an entire half of a school year is a pastime of elegance and lunacy.

The summer after kindergarten, I fell in love for the first time. Her name was Stacy, and I really had a crush on her Barbie that looked like Judy Garland from *The Wizard of Oz*. She used to carry it around like Toto in a little basket. Oh, the irony.

I'll get you, my pretty! And your little doll, too!

But I think I loved her blonde hair and beautiful dresses that she wore even more. The inklings of being different were sliding in.

When summer lovin' was over, I was giddy to go back to school. In first grade, I was in Miss Michaelson's class and I was such a happy camper. She was warm and caring and frumpy and amazing, like an old maiden aunt from *The Waltons*.

My classroom became my happy place because everywhere else was not. School was only six blocks away, but they were a long six blocks. My brother the hellion used to torture me coming and going.

He still tortures me, actually.

More on that, later.

I can't really take it too personally, as he didn't save his wrath for me, alone. He was an equal opportunity offender, delighting in driving my mother absolutely insane. Sometimes, he'd be able to exasperate both of us at the same time, which I have to admit was impressive.

He used to like hitting me for every reason and no reason while he thought my mother was too busy driving the car to care. Eventually, his annoying taps would turn into outright hostility and craziness, which was really not too bright in a small moving car.

After one too many hits, my mom would unload… literally. She would stop the '62 Chevy Impala with the baby-blue plastic-covered seats, and kick him out of the car. Once he was out, she'd hit the gas… the inertia slamming the car door closed as she sped away.

This, of course, would send my sister into hysterics thinking that he would either die on the side of the road, or we'd never see him again. But I'd seen my mother's modus operandi with my father, so I knew what was up.

I tried to calm my sister down by saying, "Oh don't worry. She's just going to drive around the block a few times and then pick him up."

And true to form… she did just that.

I was becoming more aware that life wasn't easy for my mom. She was twenty-five years old, had three children, no experience, and no one to really help her. My father was busy building a nest egg for all of us, and his hours were abnormally long. And when he was around, which was not very often, he was always visiting his parents.

Of course, when you have a relationship like he had with my mom, I can't say that I blamed him. He just had this connection with his mom and dad that was like no other. When you realize the hardships they had survived together, what would you expect? For a long time though, I could not understand.

I remember I called him on it once when I was a teenager.

"Why do you spend more time with them than us?" I asked.

"Because they're more important," he said. "My parents will always come first, and you just have to understand that."

I'm not sure if he meant it as it sounded, and I can say that about most of the things that my parents said. I don't think of them as vicious or mean-spirited. This is just what life was for them.

I learned to forgive him eventually, but not that day. When those words left his lips, there was nothing more to say.

Subconsciously, I think my home life finally started to bleed into my school life. In second grade, I had Miss Coyle. She had her hair parted to the side, behind her ear, and short, just like Barbra Streisand in *Funny Girl*. I was thrilled to be in her class.

One day, Miss Coyle asked me to read aloud. I don't remember what we were reading, but instead of saying the word "island," I pronounced it "is-land." Well, the other kids thought this was the funniest thing they'd heard in a long time, and they started making fun of me for what seemed like forever.

My reaction to the teasing was probably not my smartest decision because when they saw how much it affected me, they teased me harder. It was like *Lord of the Flies* on steroids.

Lily Tomlin said that the exact same thing happened to her on one of her comedy albums. At least I wasn't the only one on my is-land.

I couldn't shake the teasing because I couldn't shake the way it made me feel. It made me think that I was stupid, and it changed me. Miss

Coyle tried to get me past it by having me read aloud again and again, but I refused, which did not bode well for my grade.

She gave me a D in reading. Who the hell gets a D in 2nd grade? Oh… that's right. I did.

I can't say I expected the grade, and Miss Coyle tried to give me every out. But even had I known the full magnitude of the consequences of my actions, I still think the D was preferable to the mockery.

Yet I knew that the fourth letter of the alphabet would go over like a lead balloon with my parents, so I stupidly tried to trick them by changing the letter grade on the paper from a D to a B. My artistic skills failed me miserably and I couldn't make it believable.

The lack of effort continued to my homework, as I started lying about even having any to my folks. The truth is, I was scared to even try. I thought I was stupid, and if I really was, what was the point of trying?

I had to face facts… I was just different from everyone else, and not in a good way. Second grade was the last time I would be happy in school. For a while, at least.

And what do people do when they're unhappy? They become comics. If I couldn't be the smart kid, I was going to be the funny kid… which is not altogether smart.

So there I was, being my own self-fulfilling prophecy.

Oy!

# 5

# Amanda

After the horror show of second grade reading, third grade became
one of the great dichotomies of my life. We had a teacher named
Mrs. Wexler, a fashionista who wore all her gray hair stacked like Marge
Simpson on top of her head and wore form-fitting wraparound dresses,
which were huge at the time. They became fashionable again a few years
ago. She was Jewish and drove an Impala.

I don't necessarily remember her so much for her looks, but rather for
the life lesson she revealed to me. I didn't think she was overly special,
until the day she started reading *Charlie and the Chocolate Factory* to the class.
She was very expressive and had a different voice for each character. It
was an epiphany to see Mrs. Wexler leave herself to become so many
other personalities. It gave me my first inclination of what it was like to
change who you are, and it was the start of my mission to take her
example and make it something that I could not only imitate, but make my
own. In other words, it was my first glimpse of seeing myself as a
character actor.

Maybe school wasn't such a bad thing.

And then again…

I've often heard the saying, "If a girl is mean to you, it means she likes
you." If that's the case, a girl named Mala must have wanted me badly in
third grade. Once, for absolutely no reason, she punched me on the nose.

I mean dead center. The next day, I looked like Marcia "Oh my nose!" Brady. My mother made me go to the hospital because it swelled up.

When I arrived, they checked me in. My mom told me that I was just going to look at the room, and that I wouldn't have to stay there, which wasn't really the truth.

I wasn't so much mad at her lie as I was scared at the whole situation. I shared the room with a baby who was in an oxygen tent. His whole family was there during the day, and they were all dressed up like they had just come from a Baptist church revival. And when some family members had to leave, others arrived in their place.

I had not had much experience with African Americans at that time, but the love that this family had for each other profoundly affected me. At all times of the day, they came to support this little baby fighting for his life. It was quite a bit different than just my mom and my grandmother Molly sitting by my side, which meant the world to me, nonetheless.

After a couple of days in the hospital, I woke up to find that the baby was gone. No one would tell me whether he had gotten better or if he died, but I felt this incredible sense of being alone. I still think of him every now and then whenever I think about my own family.

Like many moments in my life, I never told anyone else that the punch happened. Why would I? It's one thing to get punched in the nose by a boy. A girl doing it, forget about it... my reputation would be ruined!

Reputation? Who was I kidding?

Mala almost made me swear off any interest in girls for the rest of my life. Hah!

Continuing with my loss of self-esteem. My fourth grade teacher, Mrs. Shambard, could never remember my name! She wasn't a bad person by any stretch of the imagination, but yes! She always forgot my name. Apparently I reminded her of a boy named Spencer.

So Spencer I was. So be it.

Just when I thought my nose had healed and I was more or less whole again... or as whole as I ever felt... a few years slogged by and sixth grade happened, and everything I thought I knew flipped upside down.

Mrs. Garris was our teacher. She was this stunningly beautiful black woman who wore these fashionable maxi-coats that would go down to the floor. Whenever she'd put any of her coats in the cloak closet, she would delicately pin construction paper to the fabric so that our grubby sixth grade hands wouldn't get them dirty.

She was definitely one of those teachers who the dads would volunteer at school just to get a glimpse of her radiance; she was really breathtaking. I didn't so much have a crush on her as I was simply drawn to her, much like I was drawn to all things beautiful.

It also helped that she made me the bell ringer of the class, which was a very important job that most of the kids wanted. But it was mine, and I was thrilled.

Sadly, the new name didn't give me new self-esteem. I remember we had to give an oral history presentation, and we were supposed to invite our parents in to see it. I could have chosen something close to our family, like World War II and the Holocaust, but I didn't. Instead, I did a report on toy-making in Japan. My parents looked at me like I had three heads... which might have made things more normal.

Yet as loathsome as the year could and probably should have been, there was a star in my universe of darkness...

... and her name was Amanda.

She was new, and definitely not like the other girls. She was not into being a good girl or daddy's princess. She was tough, smart, and had an air that said, I don't give a shit what you think of me. But I'm totally cool and you need to know me.

Her confidence enveloped me, almost as if it was enough for both of us. It was the first time in my life when I thought I might need to get my act together and find a girl to fall in love with. I needed her to help me start my heterosexuality. As far as I was concerned, "That's the girl I'm going to marry!"

Amanda's parents were divorced. Her dad was a big time television director, with credits like *Fame*, *The Love Boat*, and *Matlock* to his name. I would only find this out later in our relationship. Her mother had gotten remarried... this time to a very wealthy lawyer named Saul.

They had a beautiful Spanish house near the Gardner Library. I can't tell you the number of times I rode my bike there through the years. On nice days (which is almost every day in Los Angeles), Amanda and I would ride around her neighborhood, fantasizing about which nice house would be ours. And, of course, it would all be okay because she was Jewish, like me.

Actually, let's back up a second. Technically, Amanda was half-Jewish. Her biological dad was not, but her mother, Nina, was. But truth be told, if your mother's Jewish, you're all Jewish.

Well, that's what they say... whoever they are.

Not that it mattered. I learned very early on that thinking less of someone because of faith or skin color or if they had green hair made very little sense to me. Once, I was sitting with my cousin, Mitch, watching TV. I was six, and I remember that it was some sort of holiday because all of our families were hanging out together. We were watching *I Love Lucy* on a Magnavox portable television. He pointed to her and said, "That's Lucy."

"Is she Jewish?" I asked.

"No," he replied. "She's not one of the chosen people. We're the chosen people."

At that moment, my parents and his parents were in the background having this huge argument about... something... and I remember looking at them and thinking, 'Oh my God, are those crazy nutcases the chosen people?'

From that day on, at the age of six, I made the decision that I was never going to like or dislike someone because they were or weren't Jewish. I would judge each person individually, because as the show said, I loved Lucy. I couldn't imagine that she wasn't chosen!

Chosen or not, my mother loved Amanda. Maybe it was her free spirit. Maybe it was her confidence. Maybe it was the appearance that her son was happy and somewhat stable in this relationship with a pretty girl. Thanks to a nightmare school existence and an increasingly insane home life comprised of parents who couldn't stand each other, a brother who spent hours coming up with new and inventive ways of torturing me, and a sister who was daddy's little girl, Amanda was my saving grace.

The only time my mother was not a fan of Amanda's was every time she had to use the phone. This may come as a shock to some of you, but when I was growing up, we had to get by on one telephone line. For five people.

And it was attached to the wall! Oy!

Amanda and I would spend hours on the phone talking about absolutely everything from music to art, to books and movies, to nothing in particular. Sometimes, we'd go through long stretches of not even saying anything… it was simply enough to feel her connection through the line. Of course, this connection would routinely be broken by my delicate flower of a mother yelling, "Oh for Christ's sake, get off the phone! I need to make a call! I live here, too!"

Amanda's mom was a different story. For starters, she could not have been more polar opposite of Gloria. She was a dancer and artist of sorts, and she didn't like me very much. I think she thought me odd, which, of course, I was.

Too chatty, too loud, just too much!

To be honest though, I'm possibly not being fair. I thought everyone saw me as odd back then. My feelings on her feelings may not be based in any reality. I know… shocker.

Their house near the Gardner Library was everything ours was not. It had style and class and taste. The beautiful, earthy, real-wood tables with the simple tasteful china were so striking.

We, on the other hand, had a white wraparound couch that was covered in plastic. It was paired with a silver lamé and glass-top coffee table. One year while watching the Emmys, Cher came out on stage. My brother was somehow affected seeing her belly button that he dropped the top of a candy jar on the table, breaking the glass.

My mother never forgave him. Of course, I'm not sure I have either. The burden of holding the grudge is made easier by the fact that he was an asshole about everything... even when he was defending my idol. When Glenda Jackson's performance in *A Touch of Class* beat out Barbra Streisand's in *The Way We Were* for the Oscar, he barked, "She isn't even an American!"

Damn right, she's not!

Wait, what does that have to do with anything?

Yet even though my life was anything but stable, I didn't shy away from new things. Quite the contrary, really; I was drawn to new experiences and sights and smells and tastes. And it wasn't just Amanda's house that gave me new perspectives. In a sense, I was surrounded by them.

I used to hang out at my friend Freddy's house. They had a maid named Marion who would serve dinner with a cigarette hanging out of her mouth. His mom would ring the bell, and the food would come out in these little tiny portions.

Who the hell rings a bell for dinner?

Whenever I'd come home, not only would I be starving, but I would think, 'Wow, not everyone eats like it's the last day of their life every day.'

My friend Scott introduced me to my first tree-trimming when his mom hosted a Christmas decorating party. We had quiche and salad, another first for me. Their walls were bright green with white trim, and everything was so perfectly decorated... so fresh and new, it looked like a show I saw on TV. Ours looked like a TV house, too... *Married With Children.*

If Al and Peg were Jewish. And Jewish. And tackier.

I dug Scott's mom. Actually, I dug all my friends' moms, and I constantly fell for them. My friend Alan's mom, Reva, was one of my favorites. She was everything I could have ever wanted in a woman... if only I wanted a woman. And she lived right across the street, so any time I needed a fix, I popped over.

My friend Alan was a beautifully sweet blonde boy whom everyone liked. In hindsight, he was really my first crush. At that time, I didn't understand all the feelings I had, but I was obsessed with him. He and I, along with our friend Randy, used to ride bikes like it was our occupation. Randy and I would always fight to see who would be second when we were riding them in a row.

There I go again… fighting for second place. Though in this case, second place would be first place because it meant being closer to Alan. Sometimes, I was second. And sometimes, my nemesis Randy beat me to it.

Curse you, Randy!

My reality was that I was in love with Alan, though not in any kind of a sexual way; it was in that way that almost every boy experiences once in his life. Alan was that friend who I always wanted to be around.

And it didn't matter where we hung out, as long as it was away from my deteriorating reality. My home life, which had never been like the TV show *Family* with Kristy McNichol, was rapidly becoming like the TV show *Medical Center*, without the illness… physically, anyway.

Rodney Dangerfield once joked about walking in on his wife while she was being intimate with their milkman, and then she made him promise not to tell their butcher.

I don't know what Rodney's butcher's name was, but our butcher's name was George. And he and my mother had an affair for fifteen of her twenty-two-year marriage. To add insult to injury, my father actually walked in on them once. I think deep down that my mother was relieved that the cat was out of the bag. She had wanted out of her marriage from the time she said "I do."

On the other hand, George did give my mom lots of free meat.

The jokes… they write themselves.

After being caught, Gloria saw it as her escape; she was ready to bolt without passing Go or collecting two hundred dollars. Her parents stood in her way. They were old school, and divorce was something you just didn't do. To top it off, my father was "a very good provider," and that was reason enough to stay together.

So they did... for a while.

But as bad as things were at home, they were even more unbearable at school.

In seventh grade, I went to John Burroughs Junior High School. When I first arrived, they gave me a locker that would be mine for the duration of my time there. Someone took a nail and scratched the word Fag onto the outside of the door. Every time I twisted my combination lock and opened it, there it was. I endured it every day for three years and never told a soul.

Once on the bus ride home, I was pushed around like a football by some of the bigger kids. People were calling me "fag" and "queer," which always hurt tremendously. I never really knew what the words meant, except that I must have been wrong or bad to be called either of those names.

I got off the bus, and my friend Loretta got off at the same time. She came over to see if I was okay, and I remember being barely able to breathe or even look at her as I failed to hold it together under the crushing weight of so much humiliation. As she tried to speak, I barked at her, "Don't touch me!"

"I'm not," she said, "I'm just..."

"I'm sorry! I just can't!" I screamed.

And I ran away. I was so shell-shocked by my outburst. The rage and pain and angst had built, and I finally exploded all over poor Loretta. I'm grateful that years later, I was given the opportunity to apologize to her.

But school and home aside, not even my faith, or lack thereof, was a safe place for me.

When I was thirteen, I had my bar mitzvah. The ceremony is a rite-of-passage... when a boy becomes a man in the Jewish faith tradition. I would have to perform the Torah, or a reading from the prophets. I practiced, but I remember telling the rabbi, "I don't know what any of this means."

"You don't need to know what any of it means," he responded. "You just need to shut up and do it."

Not only that, but this holy man would not even let me write my own speech. I had to use my brother's, which I'm sure instilled a particular glee in my nemesis knowing that each of the words that came out of my mouth were his, first. Each syllable tasted like pure vinegar to me.

Thanks God. Why have you forsaken me on my special day? You're probably busy somewhere on cable TV. We, of course, don't have cable. Every time I ask, my dad says, "What do we need that for?!"

Maybe for times like this, Dad! Oy!

And I was such a bad Hebrew School student that I did all of my parts in the ceremony phonetically. I had not a freaking clue what was going on. I might as well have been one of the kids in *The Partridge Family*.

"Wait, what are we supposed to lip sync?"

It doesn't matter!

I don't remember any words from the ceremony, but I do remember that Amanda bought me Carole King's album *Tapestry*. I played it over and over again because I loved the music… and because I loved Amanda, or as much as I could love Amanda.

I also remember everyone remarking what a great couple we were. Little did I know that our "couple-hood" would soon be over… impossible to consummate, no matter how hard I tried.

We had our first boy-girl party together soon after. At some point during the revelry, she cast me aside and ended up kissing this boy named Simeon. I was pretty shaken up by it. This was my confidant, my friend, my ally, my quasi-girlfriend, and she cheated. In my house!

I wonder if this was how my dad felt.

A few days after that, I walked her home and said, "I'm breaking up with you."

She thought I had some nerve. She screamed a dirty word or two, and I retorted with, "Well there's plenty of other fish in the sea!"

Not that I had much to do with it, but Amanda changed a little after that. Never one to blend in with the crowd in our class, she found herself going down the rabbit hole more and more. I don't know how long it took me to see it, but Amanda had become the *Go Ask Alice* of our class. A popular book about a teenager who dies of drug abuse.

It all came to a head in eighth grade. She'd been cutting classes on a regular basis and had all but given up on school. This had not gone unnoticed by one of the administrators, Mr. Egglestein. He was prissy and uptight, and always wore a bowtie. His balding head and little round glasses reminded me of every stereotypical teacher in a 1960's movie.

Mr. Egglestein tried to get through to her to help her in his own uptight way. She told him to "go fuck himself." I saw it unfold in disbelief, right before my eyes.

And then, Amanda... my ex-girlfriend... walked out of school.

And then she was promptly kicked out of school, meaning the effective end of her academic career, which was just fine by her. She got in with some bad people and into some bad habits... a.k.a. drugs. She would disappear for great lengths of time, and her mother would constantly call me to ask where she was.

I had no idea where she was. But while I was a little worried, I also knew that she would find a way to survive. It's who she was at her core.

She always kept in touch on her time. She'd call throughout our high school years, or rather, my high school years. We met up once at Will Rogers State Park in Malibu in tenth grade. She had plucked her eyebrows really thin and her hair was long and lightened by the sun from hitchhiking, which made her an even more striking vision.

She had a style all her own... pulling off the look of a 1970's California hip chick you'd see in a film with Steve McQueen or Ryan O'Neal. And I was still attracted to being around her, if not quite attracted to her. She was magnetic... effortlessly radiating her I still don't give a shit what you think of me vibe.

Another time, I picked her up on La Cienega Boulevard. She was wearing jeans and a tank top with airbrushing on it. She looked thin and gorgeous and cool and hip, as usual. She spent much of the time smoking cigarettes and constantly telling me how she was going to get her life together.

And she talked about how she wanted to be like me, all settled down with goals and dreams and aspirations. If she'd only known how much I wanted to be like her... to let loose and not care what people thought of me.

Once, we decided that we would try going steady one last time. It lasted all of about a hot minute. One afternoon, she and I were in my room at my parents' house. I was sixteen and feeling it, so I pushed her down on my bed. We kissed passionately for a few seconds before stopping, looked deeply into each other's eyes, and burst out in laughter.

"This is not going to work," she giggled.

"It was kind of like kissing a family member," I said.

It was then that I knew deep in my heart that no woman was ever going to be able to fulfill my desires... to make me feel the way I did when I rode bikes with Alan and Randy.

Not even Amanda, my eternal *Go Ask Alice* hero.

# 6

## Sadie, Sadie

I t's amazing the good that can come out of the bad. For instance, as sometimes morbidly terrible as junior high was, some pretty fantastic things began to percolate to the surface of my life. Our school was putting on a production of *Harvey*, and I really wanted a part in the play. Of course, my self-worth was in the toilet, so I auditioned for the part of the cab driver and not the lead.

Hey, I was happy I auditioned. Baby steps.

Imagine my shock when I actually landed the part. I hadn't been in a school play since I played Geppetto in a grammar school production of *Pinocchio*. I was going to nail it.

During rehearsals, a girl in my class named Lise took an interest in my performance. She was from the wrong side of the tracks of Beverly Hills... in other words, the apartments across Wilshire Boulevard. Sad to say, I would love to live there at this point in my life, but c'est la vie.

One day, she told me, "You look faggy on stage."

She couldn't have stopped those baby steps any better than if she took a tack hammer and nailed my feet to the floor. To be fair, I don't think she meant it to be disrespectful or hurtful or malicious. It was probably an off-handed comment that meant nothing to her, but it meant everything to me.

And with that critique, it was the second... and last... school play that

I ever did. My acting would have to be limited to the West Side Jewish Center and the Los Angeles Parks and Recs, where I could be relatively anonymous when I starred in classics like *Snarf, David and Goliath*, and *The Birds.*

I played the Tippi Hedren character. Kidding!

I also got the lead role in *Santa Claus for President.* I played the entire part as if I was Lucille Ball, pregnant. In other words, I wore a fat suit. I got tons of laughs, and I remember everyone coming up to compliment me. The director of the play, Meyer Levine, said to me, "You're gonna do this, aren't you? You're gonna be an actor."

I looked at him, and for the first time out loud, I said, "Yes."

So I thought that until I became a star, I could sell maps to stars' homes. At least it would keep me in the neighborhood. I worked the corner of Bronson and Sunset...

... no, not like that... I was thirteen, people...

... and after a couple of weeks of my high-energy salesmanship, I was cleaning up. Just when things were going exceptionally well, these two transvestites got into a massive bitch-fight on my corner. One was wearing a perm-wig, platforms, a halter top, and hot pants that looked like something my mom would wear. And they were beating the shit out of each other. With so many kicks and Lee Press-On-Nails flying, I'm shocked nothing extracurricular popped out during the melee. I quit that very day and never went back.

Around the same time, a reporter on a TV show called *PM Magazine* did a profile on a folk singer named Carney, who was transgender. I really connected with Carney, as she said so many of the same things I felt. But I thought to myself, 'While I relate to Carney emotionally, I'm still attached to my penis.' I didn't want to be a woman... I just wanted a man.

Oy! Where do I fit in?

Thanks to Carney and the bitch-fight, I thought that it would be best if I suppressed my feelings... hoping they would go away. Of course I knew they wouldn't, and I have to say it was an incredibly low point in my life. It was at that moment that the universe intervened to show me that no matter what, "Everything was going to be okay."

In 1971, there was an ABC movie called *That Certain Summer* starring Hal Holbrook and Hope Lange (who starred in *The Ghost and Mrs. Miller*). I had received a very small television as a bar mitzvah present, and in those days, the smaller the TV, the cooler it was. And just the fact that a thirteen-year-old had something so technologically advanced in his bedroom impressed me (and no one else) so much.

As I watched the preview for *That Certain Summer* on that little TV sitting on my desk, Hope belted out the line about how if he was a woman, she would know how to compete.

The moment I heard her terror-filled angst, I knew I was supposed to watch that movie. Holbrook plays a man who moves from Los Angeles to San Francisco to manage a construction company. He ends up living in this apartment with his lover, a handsome man played by Martin Sheen… the president from *West Wing*.

There's a scene where Holbrook helps Sheen pack his stuff up because he has to go stay with his sister for the summer. At the same time, Holbrook's son, Scott Jacoby (who won the Emmy for his portrayal), is coming over to the apartment so that his dad can tell him he's gay… hence, *That Certain Summer*.

In that scene, both Holbrook and Sheen are wearing sweaters, which made me think that for a man to be gay, he had to wear a sweater. In one of the pivotal moments, Sheen puts his hand on Holbrook and says that everything will be okay.

At least, that's the way I remember it.

I'd never seen two men touch… wearing men's clothes. I just about died. It was the first inkling I had experienced that, indeed, a man could love another man.

And then to confirm it, I looked up homosexuality in the World Book Encyclopedia… what today is called the Internet… and next to the word homosexual, it read mentally ill.

In fact, the mainstream understanding of homosexuality was so primitive that it took until 1973 for the American Psychiatry Association to say that gay people weren't, in fact, mentally ill.

I slammed the book shut.

Hello, ten years of therapy!

One of the things that always helped me keep my sanity in those dark days was music. I used to frequent a record store called The Frigate on 3rd Street quite a bit to buy my forty-fives… or as I like to call it, the early seventies version of iTunes. I would ride my bike there, park it in front, and get lost in the rows and rows of vinyl.

A woman named Joan used to work there part-time. She was the first lesbian I ever met, and at first, I actually thought she was a man. She wore men's tailored shirts, jeans, and comfortable shoes. She was gruff by all accounts, and yet I was drawn to her. Beneath the exterior, she really had an inviting presence, and I was completely enamored.

I had never met anyone like Joan, and I knew that I needed to know her better. I would get the chance when I went to work for her.

Joan was also a bit of an entrepreneur, and right next to the record store, she opened up a place called Sadie. It was a mish-mash of a boutique; you could buy plants, cards, and gifts. Soon after opening, you could also buy a cup of coffee and children's toys. It really offered the coolest things.

I ended up getting hired as a stock boy. It was the first job that I really cared about, but it wasn't my actual first job. That honor goes to Jack in the Box. The manager handed me a foreign object and said, "Mop the floor."

"I live three blocks from Beverly Hills, I don't mop floors," I replied.

I thought it was hilarious; the manager didn't. Needless to say, my job ceased to exist precisely fourteen seconds after my little outburst.

I worked at Sadie for years, and I absolutely loved it. I was unafraid of hard work… one of the traits my father instilled in me. That job also taught me a valuable lesson I would take with me for life: if you love what you do, then work really isn't work.

It also didn't hurt that the name of the store came from a song in *Funny Girl*. Called *Sadie, Sadie*.

I could listen to that song all day. Maybe I could play it at my wedding… if I ever find a good guy to marry me!

Joan's girlfriend was a gal named Dena. She was pretty and flighty and had a big Jew-fro. When she was done with her own job, she would come in and play songs on her guitar while sitting at the back of the store.

What made her even more intriguing was that she was a TV actress when she was a kid. I was so sold on Dena. Just being around her meant I had a connection to where I wanted to go, even though she hadn't worked in the business since she was young. That was good enough for me.

Dena became one of my all-time favorite people. Her kindness was just what the doctor ordered. She and I would literally talk for hours as I would dust and price items and open up cardboard boxes. Joan was not thrilled with my performance because she thought I should be doing my job.

And they never looked down on me. They never asked me if I was gay, and we never talked about being gay. They just treated me like I was one of them, and for the first time in a long time, I felt like I really belonged. I could be myself, whoever that person was. I was still trying to figure that out. Years later, I would call Dena to thank her for her kindness, and to help me on the path of self-awareness.

Actually, I'm still trying to find the end of that path, though I doubt I'll ever fully get to my destination.

Joan hosted anniversary parties each year for the store, and she would always invite all her lesbian friends. Every now and then, there were some gay boys who would attend, as well. I began to realize that I was not alone, or at least, I didn't have to be alone. A choice was out there somewhere, and it was liberating in one sense.

It was also confounding in another sense. Gay men used to come into the shop all the time, but I had absolutely no idea how to assimilate. I didn't know how to act, what to say, or how to embrace my feelings, so I avoided getting close to anyone but these strong lesbian women.

I was once asked by a friend if coming to terms with my sexuality was an easier evolution because I chose to associate with Joan and Dena instead of John and Dean. I think it might have been easier with women than men at that time because I could be myself without actually having to publicly admit that part of me, which I was terrified to do.

But let's face facts: unbeknownst to me, I chose to associate with women… and in this case, gay women… because I didn't know how to associate with gay men. If you were not ready to publicly own your sexuality just yet, but you hung around with gay men, people were going to think you were gay, whether you were or weren't.

And I experienced this firsthand when I became a comedian. There were some closeted comics who could not stay further away from me, lest they be labeled as gay… guilt by association… which made me so sad. It made me feel even more ostracized than I already was.

So I was too afraid to say anything, to speak up, as was the reality of the time. And in many places, it is still very much the reality. So to combat this, when I was too afraid to speak for myself, I stood behind the skirts of women, my allies, way too much, and I let them speak for me.

And the reason is that much of the world found gay men more palatable if our voices came through women. When I was growing up, we really had no voice. In my youth, I chose to just keep to myself. I didn't start getting good gay male friends until I got older, but the seed was planted in that wonderful little shop.

School continued to be rough for me. In the tenth grade at Fairfax High School, a kid named Langston socked me in the face as I was walking from P.E. to my art class, where I did all his artwork for virtually the entire semester. I think he knew how attracted I was to him, though I never dared to breathe a word.

But as my Elton John glasses flew off my face, and my friend Joey ran away… so as not to be Langston's next victim… I feigned like I was going to hit him back as I tried to stand up, but then the teachers ran over to break us up.

Thank God.

It was another day of humiliation... times ten. People have asked me if I ever got into fights in high school, and I always say, "No, but I was beaten up." I could never bring myself to hit someone back, but I knew that day what I had to do to defend myself: I was going to get out of high school as soon as possible.

For the next two and a half years, I worked like my life depended on it, and I graduated six months early. I can't say I learned very much, but because it was the 70's, dancing in a circle while wearing a tie-dye t-shirt was enough to get you a diploma.

And that is where my schooling stopped. I never went to college for the same reason why I wanted out of high school. I could not see myself being put into a school situation with people my own age. It was too frightening. Little did I know that it probably would have been the best thing for me... to be with people my own age who were going through the same thing that I was going through.

I didn't have anyone to show me the way until I met Joan. She, Dena, and Sadie, gave me a place where I could breathe.

Like so many good things in life though, my time at Sadie didn't last forever. I would get calls here and there to help out, but my job was fluid. If they didn't need me, I wouldn't show up. Eventually, Joan closed the store, and she ended up moving away to northern California. Yet thanks to her, I discovered that there was a place for people like me.

Or rather, places for people like me.

It was 1975; I was sixteen and unable to fully comprehend where my own sexual desires were going to take me. One night, they took me to the Gordon Theatre on La Brea to see a double feature of *A Woman Under the Influence* starring Gena Rowlands, and *Alice Doesn't Live Here Anymore* with Ellen Burstyn. During one of the movies, and out of the corner of my eye, I spotted a Latin man touching himself. He saw that I saw, and when the movies ended, he followed me out of the theatre. He invited me to go back to his house, which was a second floor apartment of a beautiful Spanish-style duplex located about six blocks from where I live now.

As you can tell by my recollection of his abode, I took him up on his offer.

I followed him to his place, and I remember that there was not a whole lot of talking. And before I really knew what was happening, he gave me my first blowjob.

This was the mid 70's... there was no Internet, no videos to see if what you were doing was or was not the correct or acceptable protocol, and no chat rooms. I had no idea if this guy had bad technique giving, or if I had bad technique receiving.

Yes. Seriously.

As I look back, I realize just how messed up I could have been, beyond how messed up I actually became. The ill-fated school play. The map to stars' homes. *That Certain Summer.* Joan and Dena. The Latin man in the theatre.

And all the thoughts and fears and angst took root in my mind, alone, because I told not a soul about any minor triumph or crushing defeat I experienced...

... including my naïve sexual skills, apparently.

As he went down on me, all I could think was, 'I don't like this. This is nothing. Not for me.'

So I went back the next day... just to make sure I didn't like it.

# 7

# The Last Train to Heterosexuality Stops Here

Just because I let a Latin man blow me… twice… didn't mean that I was ready to come out. With all the negative stigma around being gay in the 70's, I still thought my life would be easier if I suppressed any homosexual urges I had, and just settled down with a woman.

But who?

Amanda was more like my sister; she was my family.

Ick. Strike one.

I had already dipped my… toe… into disconnected gay sex.

Too uncomfortable. Strike two.

I was starting to get a little desperate. My friend Bobby and I decided to go to the movies one night, and I was going to make it my mission to find a girlfriend in the process.

By the way, the movie we were going to see was *A Star is Born*. Yes… the one with Barbra Streisand.

Writing themselves, these jokes are.

I drove to the theatre in my '68 rust colored Camaro with Bobby… his hair flowing with more layers than a lasagna. As we pulled up to a stoplight, I spotted a girl sitting at a bus stop. She wore a long maxi-dress with a bustier in the middle. She had a curly reddish perm and the sweetest smile. I thought, 'What could be more heterosexual than picking this girl up?'

So I flirted with her like my life depended on it because to me, it did. I never would have had the guts to put myself out like that, but Bobby was a friend, and more importantly, an audience. I think I was trying to impress him as much as I was trying to impress her.

Seeing that she was receptive to my charms, I boldly asked her to get in the car with us. She accepted the invitation.

Hey, it was the 70's... people did this all the time. Of course, little did I realize it would be one of the top two massive mistakes of my life.

Her name was Lisa, and she lived with her mom and her grandfather in a house that looked like a murder took place there thirteen years ago, and the neighbors still talked about it.

Don't go near that house!

I don't believe they owned a lawn mower, or tires for the car they had up on blocks. The first time I looked into the house, I remember seeing stacks of boxes, and through a gap in the stacks, I saw her grandfather slowly rocking back and forth in a back room while watching *Let's Make a Deal* on an old Magnavox portable TV. If I was closer, I would have put a mirror under his nose to make sure he was still alive.

Maybe he was the one murdered thirteen years ago.

The place had such a creepy vibe. On one window, there was a clump of old spaghetti that looked like someone threw a fistful of it during a fight. What got to me the most was that they never cleaned it up.

For thirteen years.

But that didn't stop me. As far as I was concerned, she was my girlfriend the second she agreed to let me pick her up.

I remember the first time I almost made it into her house. Her mother, who I believe was from somewhere in Europe, wanted to meet me. I seriously couldn't tell you where she was from, nor the dialect of her accent.

"Lizz-ah, Lizz-ah... we must have your new boyfriend in the house for tea. We must!" she implored.

Lisa was so embarrassed that she screamed, "Mother! I don't want him in the house! I can't have him in the house! Don't let him in the house!"

She reminded me of Hayley Mills in *The Chalk Garden*. "Motha! Motha!"

I eventually did meet her mom. Something was a bit off though because whenever I asked her where she was from, she would never give me a straight answer.

Ever.

It was like she was in the witness protection program.

I will say though, that this woman was very smart. She was always taking a class, or painting, or going to a ballet recital. And she was a voracious reader… which was very different than my own mom. The only book I ever saw her read was *Fear of Flying* by Erica Jong. I didn't see her read it very often, although it stayed on her nightstand for the better part of a decade. And even then, she never finished it.

Lisa took after her mom. She was smart and sweet and a diva who oozed character. And she was my girlfriend. I was so thrilled that I actually had a legitimate heterosexual girlfriend to bring to family functions.

Attending those functions was not always the most pleasant experience, however. While very smart, she was also very liberal… and an opinionated vocal liberal at that. Normally, a man would be proud to bring his aspiring doctor girlfriend to familial gatherings. I did my level best to constantly run the conversation so that she had few moments to actually speak.

It was for her own protection.

My parents were not the biggest fans of who she was, even though they liked what she was: a girl who their son was dating and, hopefully, a girl with whom he was having sex.

They got their wish on that one. Lisa was the only girl I was ever able to have sex with… to completion. And even though we did, I still didn't understand all the intricacies behind it. Or in front of it or beside it, for that matter. I'm a guy… everything's out in the open. She was a girl… and it's all on the inside. And if you can't see it...

... is it even there?

And don't get me started about going down south!

But she liked me, and more importantly, she was a girl, which was my only requirement for making this work. And besides, maybe I could learn to like it. I mean, it wasn't worse than brain surgery, even though it felt as complicated. I think I would have had an easier time with long division. But I had hope that it could get better. It would get better. And if it got better...

... my God, was this it? Was I cured?

I was now... the Daddy. (And I had the candy!). The heterosexual boyfriend!?

It would take me a long time to realize that homosexuality wasn't a disease that needed to be cured. I needed to get past my innate talent for self-loathing, but Lisa was not to be the magic potion. I think she knew who I was, but it didn't seem to bother her, at least on the surface. She would always ask me if I was gay, and of course, I always denied it.

As our relationship continued, I began having uneasy feelings about Lisa, or more specifically, her past. My mind went to places where young minds should never have to go... places where there is spaghetti on the window and it's never cleaned up... places where there are stacks of boxes in the middle of a hallway and no one ever moves them, empties them, or gets rid of them.

And what made her get into a car with two young men that night? What did she think might happen? And now just thinking about it, she had literally no reservations about her potential consequences. I mean, we were decent people, but we could have been axe murderers for all she knew.

And where was that bus taking her that night? She never did say. It could have been to the store. It could have been to run away.

I think something absolutely horrible happened to her in her past. I never had the nerve to ask her about it, whatever it was. In fact, I think if

I did ask, it would have broken her because she held it up so high, safely out of reach of anyone who dared to get too close.

As we struggled through our fifth year together, I was scrambling to grow my career. I was living on my own, and looking for any part I could muster. I saw an ad in *Variety* asking for contestants for the hottest game show on television, *The Dating Game*. I knew that if I was picked for the show, I would make union scale. So casting my excuse of a relationship aside, I applied and was selected as one of the eligible bachelors.

The bachelorette came out on stage, where she proceeded to ask multiple questions to the two other bachelors and me. I was not about to let my first appearance on television go to waste, especially since I was looking particularly fabulous that day with my layered hair and toned body.

Of course, back then I thought I was fat. My today-self would sell a kidney for my Dating Game-body, but c'est la vie.

And my answers were straight out of *A Clockwork Orange*. They had absolutely nothing to do with her questions, much to the amusement of the audience. And because I was literally so completely out of my mind...

... I won the date.

As it turns out, I was not the only struggling actor looking for a paycheck that day. The bachelorette was also a struggling actor needing to make some cash. And she had a boyfriend, who wanted nothing to do with her going out with a guy like me.

If he only knew the truth.

So she gave me the prize-winner's package of five fun-filled days in Mexico City. I thought it was the perfect, and really final, opportunity to save my dying heterosexual relationship with Lisa.

When I asked her to go, she enthusiastically said, "Yes!"

This should have been my first clue that it would be the second biggest mistake of my life.

Even though *The Dating Game* gave couples the means to have copious amounts of sex away from prying eyes, it was technically a show on a family network, so they set us up with two rooms.

This was the 70's… there was no hanky-panky on a first date!

I insisted that Lisa and I sleep in the same bed because I was supposed to be practicing my career in heterosexuality. She wouldn't let me touch her, which I have to say slightly conflicted me for about a minute.

She knew this was a last-ditch effort at a loveless relationship, and it really hurt her, so she cut off sex with me as a punishment.

Oh, the irony.

Later that afternoon, while out for a walk, we happened upon a movie set. The film was called *Missing*, directed by Costa-Gavras. It starred Jack Lemmon and Sissy Spacek, and I really wanted to watch them film it… hoping that someone on the set would look at me and say, "I want *That Girl!*"

Like the TV show starring Marlo Thomas. And then everything would freeze, and I would say, "Well, I'm a boy, not a girl, but I'm still available."

I was not prepared for Lisa's reaction.

"This reminds me of the time I was on set for my last job as a child actor on the TV show *Combat*. I hear this is violent, and I don't want anything to happen to me. Because you know, I have dancer legs."

You could have knocked me over with a feather. It made no sense, and neither did she. As I tried to work out the rationale behind her outburst, she screamed at me, "You are sooooo insensitive!"

It was that precise moment when I admitted to myself that I had been incredibly selfish, with just about everything that had to do with the girl I picked up at the bus stop. She was my last gasp at being straight, and for five years I had used her as an experiment to see if I could change.

On our last day, she had arranged for us to visit a museum to see some five hundred-year-old paintings. As we viewed the art, I noticed these two handsome Latin boys across the room. One of them looked like Esai Morales from *La Bamba* and now *Ozark*, and I could feel the perspiration start to form all over my body. He was just breathtaking, and my heart skipped a beat when I saw him.

Our chaperone from *The Dating Game*, Frankie (who became a lifelong friend), wrapped up the day by encouraging all of us to go out that evening as the entire group had gotten on so well. He told us that we should keep an open mind to new experiences as he gave us the address to a gay bar. I was giddy... awash in the possibilities.

Lisa wanted to rip my fucking head off.

I told her she didn't have to go, but she felt like making sure I had a lousy time with Ritchie Valens' older, hotter brother. She wouldn't miss this for the world.

On the way to the bar, all I could think about was the boy. I couldn't remember his name or anything either of us said, but it just felt right... pure... and real. I had never had that feeling before. I still get goosebumps thinking of the anticipation.

Only, it was not to be. I waited for hours, but he never showed up. I danced with Lisa for the very last time ever that night.

And on that dance floor, in a country where I could not speak the language, I finally accepted my fate.

I was gay.

Strike three.

When we got home, I dropped Lisa off at her house in the same '68 Camaro I picked her up in five years earlier.

I never expected to see her again...

... but fifteen years ago, I ran into her at a restaurant called Souplantation in West Hollywood. She walked over to my table like we had seen each other the day before.

"We've seen you on TV," she barked... almost as if it was an accusation. "So you're an actor now."

"Uh... yes. Yes, you're right."

"Well, I'm a doctor now," she said.

"Lisa," I said, "I've always wanted to apologize to you."

"For what?"

"I'm gay."

She took a pause, and she choked back a tear.

"I KNEW IT!!!"

# 8

# Shelley Winters Changed My Name

My old neighborhood looks nothing like it does today. In the late 70's, the corner of Wilshire and Fairfax was anchored by a gigantic May Company Department Store that took up the entire corner. May is long gone, but because the building is considered historic, it's not allowed to be torn down. Instead, they're using the bones of it for the new Hollywood Museum.

It was in this neighborhood where I would wander and dream of being in show business, wishing I had some powerful long-lost relative who held a lofty position in one of the main studios. Sadly, this was not the case, so I did what every other up-and-not-yet-coming actor did: I made Schwab's Pharmacy my second home.

Located on the corner of Sunset and Crescent Heights, Schwab's was a drugstore that actually had a coffee shop in it, which was a very popular concept in those days. You could go in for pancakes, coffee, and a valium prescription in one fell swoop. It was also the place to be seen, as it was frequented by everyone from day-players to bona fide movie stars.

Everyone would go there for breakfast and lunch, and it was always crowded. All the out-of-work actors, both famous and not, were there to share who was casting what, or who was directing the next big film. Of course, these were the days when there was no Internet or smartphones, so you actually had to talk to people.

There was also another facet that virtually forced you to interact with the people around you. As it was always so hard to find a table, you sat where there was room. If a four-top table had three patrons, you became their fourth. It was like a German beer hall, without the beer.

Of course I knew all of this, and I used it to my advantage. One day, I went in for lunch hoping to be discovered, as usual. On this exceptionally crowded day, I spotted a table with two-time Academy Award winner Shelley Winters, and Sally Kirkland before she was nominated for an Oscar for her work in Anna. While she was not quite at Shelley's status, success-wise, she had already been in two movies with Barbra Streisand, as well as *The Sting* with Robert Redford and Paul Newman. Also sitting at the table was a local TV talk show host named Skip E. Lowe, who reminded me of what a lesbian leprechaun might look like.

I didn't know the fourth person at the table, which probably meant that he was just there for a quick club sandwich before going back to work. Something told me that I could get that seat if I just held out long enough.

So as people came up to be seated behind me in line, I purposely let them go in front of me while I waited for my chance. After what seemed like an eternity, and just as I'd planned, the fourth at Shelley and Sally's table paid his tab and left. It was go time.

I couldn't believe my good fortune as I sat down next to two people I really admired... and Skip. I could barely catch my breath, which was probably a good thing because none of them said a word to me for ten minutes. They were engrossed in a deep conversation about a young actress named Meryl Streep who was starring in *The Deer Hunter* with Robert De Niro. Exhausting their thoughts on the subject, Shelley looked at me and said, "So who are you?"

"Uh, my name is Stuart Greif."

"Stuart what?"

"Yes, that's my name. Stuart Ted Greif."

"Well," said Shelley in a very in-the-know Hollywood way, "that's a stupid name for a cute kid."

It was the first time when someone that famous acknowledged my existence. All I could think was, 'She said I was cute!' The fact that she called my name "stupid" flew right past me.

"I agree," said Sally... nibbling on a piece of American cheese. She hung on Shelley's every word as if she was the Queen of the United States.

Skippy put his two cents in, but his mouth was full and I couldn't understand a single word he uttered, apart from echoing Shelley's words, "cute kid."

Oh my God... had I just been discovered at Schwab's by a movie star?

Shelley and I hit it off that day. In what was such a kind gesture, she invited me to be an observer at The Actors Studio. I'm not sure what it was, specifically, that she saw in me, but I think she knew that I needed a few kind words, as well as the opportunity to see some of the most brilliant actors of the time at work. In the year-plus that I attended, Oscar winners Martin Landau, Lee Grant, and even the great Lee Strasberg, himself, moderated the sessions. It was a master class every time I went.

A few months later, I got my first-ever paying role as a professional actor. It was a nighttime comedy soap opera called *The Life and Times of Eddie Roberts* or *L.A.T.E.R.*, starring Renny Temple and Billy Barty. As thrilling as it was to see my name, Stuart Greif, roll in the end credits, I was horrified to see that they misspelled it; my first real job... credited as Stuart Grief. It brought back a flood of painful memories. I thought of the bullies growing up who used to pick on me and yell, "Good grief, it's Greif!" as they tormented me. I also thought of lunch that day with Shelley.

Cute kid. Stupid name. The next day, I changed it.

I picked the name Jason because of a popular television show at the time called *Here Come the Brides*. In the show, there were three ridiculously handsome brothers whose parents died in Seattle at the turn of the century. The oldest brother, Jason, had this wonderful paternal quality as he cared for his two younger siblings, which I had never had as a child growing up. So I decided to use his name, and transform my first name into my last name.

My dad told me that I should use my middle name and call myself Ted Stuart, but I thought it sounded too much like Ted Knight from *The Mary Tyler Moore Show*, and I thought that people might think I was stupid because we shared the same first name. It's only later in my acting career that I realized how it took an extreme amount of intelligence to play the character of "Ted Baxter" so well.

The other two brothers in *Here Come the Brides*, Jeremy and Joshua, were played by Bobby Sherman, who was a really a big heartthrob at the time, and David Soul, who became an even bigger heartthrob from *Starsky & Hutch*. And Robert Brown, who played Jason, ended up being the least successful of the bunch, as he stopped acting in 1994.

And that's who I chose for my name. Oy!

# 9

## Comedy Isn't Always Pretty

In 1983, I had a manager named Cathryn Jaymes. At that time, I was acting in a scene from a play called *Bad Habits* by Terrence McNally at a local actors' showcase, where I played the husband of a too-rich socialite played by actress Louise-Diana. You know, like Ann-Margaret.

The scene went over well, getting plenty of laughs. In fact, my ability to elicit laughter from an audience made me realize that my dream of being Timothy Hutton in *Ordinary People* was going to have to be put on hold. People thought I was funny; that was my ace in the hole.

Of course, being talented and being successful don't always go hand-in-hand. I always thought that when people would see my work, and they saw that it was good, they would want to hire me. Well that didn't happen, but it never dissuaded me from working hard.

After being featured in this showcase, I called every single agent and manager who came to see it. The only one who would meet with me was Cathryn Jaymes. The others gave me a variety of excuses.

"You're special. We're not looking for special."

"When you get older, that's when you'll work."

"The role of John Ritter is already cast."

But Cathryn didn't give me an excuse. She told me that the reason she represented me was because I wanted it so bad. This would become a recurring theme in my career.

I remember visiting casting directors' offices and having them look at me as if they had put a hand in front of my face. It didn't matter what I did... they just didn't see me. Laurence Olivier once said, "The worst thing you can do is to show someone your talent, and for them not to be able to see it."

That was my life.

And they wanted nothing to do with me, saying that I was "light in the loafers," or that "your slip is showing." These were the terms that they used in the 80's for saying that I came off as too gay.

And it wasn't just too gay. I was always too... something. I was just trying to figure out where I fit in, who I was, what was my type, so that I could just get a job. Most of the time, I was not judged on my overall talent or my ability to make people laugh or my acting talent. I was judged for being gay, and I was dismissed.

What they couldn't deny though, was my tenacity, my dedication, and my hard work.

Every acting coach I ever had tried to get me to be more masculine. My first coach, Lawrence Parke, always used to say, "Anchor your hands! Anchor your hands!"

He would have us do these great improvisations that were both comedic and dramatic. In those scenes, we would play actions, create sense memories, and become characters. If I was funny in a scene, he would shout out, "Bar Stool! Bar Stool!"

I was fourteen... I had no clue what the hell "bar stool" meant.

As an admitted bisexual, I really believe Larry was trying to help me. He didn't want me to achieve the lack of success he endured. His career highlight as an actor was playing the mailman on *The Real McCoys* with Oscar winner Walter Brennan. He figured that being gay halted his career, and he wanted to protect me.

"What does 'bar stool' mean?" I asked.

"You look like a gay guy sitting on a bar stool making rude comments and getting laughs," he said. "That will never get you a job."

Thank God he was so wrong… that's totally why my early career took off.

But he continued to work with me. When I asked him why he gave me the opportunity in the first place, he gave me the same reason as Cathryn: "Because you wanted it so bad."

I had a casting director friend named Jackie Burch who cast me in some of my first films, including *Kindergarten Cop* and *Vegas Vacation*. She would always tell me to butch it up before I came in for an audition. She, too, had my best interests at heart.

One day while making the rounds at Universal Studios, I thought I'd take her advice. As I showed up to her office to drop off my updated résumé and head shot, I strode in as if I was in a western starring John Wayne.

"Jason, what are you doing?" she laughed. "You look like you've just gotten off a horse!"

"Great! That's what I was going for!" I said.

She just looked at me as if I was crazy, and I loved her for it. We're still dear friends to this day.

Seeing my ability to make people laugh, Cathryn was the first person who told me I should do stand-up comedy. We talked about it a lot during that period, as I wound up working at her office part-time, which seemed like the only way I could get interviews for parts. I also helped her keep things together when they would fall apart… which happened more than I can say. She had a bit of a drinking and spending problem. But I stuck with her because she stuck with me… and because one of her biggest clients was E. J. Peaker, who starred in *Hello, Dolly!* with Barbra Streisand. If she was good enough for E.J., she was good enough for me!

So she set up an audition for me at The Comedy Store in May of 1983. I was to go on before Damon Wayans… just a year before his first role in *Beverly Hills Cop* as the "Banana Man."

I went onstage with a bathroom scale around my neck, spouting a lot of fat jokes about when I was a kid. I was so nervous, but I got laughs. I wasn't made a regular, and I didn't get my name on the wall that night; it would take seven more years for that to happen.

But it was a beginning.

Soon, I would be considered a non-paid regular, which meant that I could call them and say, "An industry professional wants to see me," which would afford me a guest spot on any given night.

My second show was at The Improv. I followed Billy Crystal... seriously... and I absolutely bombed.

Seriously.

I just wasn't able to re-create the same ball of kinetic nervous energy that I had pulled off at The Comedy Store. I still got a few laughs, but it felt different. It was different.

It took me another eight years to get back to The Improv as a regular performer.

With a short string of maybes and almosts in my pocket, and in true Jason Stuart fashion, I put my nose to the grindstone and made it a rule that I would do stand-up three times per week, no matter what. And that's what I did all over LA, until I got my first real paying gig as the opening act at a Mexican-Irish restaurant in La Verne, California called Carlos O'Brien's. I performed in a carpeted barbecue pit. Before that night, I didn't know carpeted barbecue pits even existed.

My second barely-paying job was in Palm Springs, California at The Comedy Haven, which was run by this tough gal named Phyllis Silver who used to be the accountant at The Comedy Store in Hollywood. She reminded me a little of Barbara Stanwyck... tough, but no heart. Phyllis put me up in the comedy condo, which was a two-bedroom apartment five minutes from the club. The house comedian was a drag queen who closed her act every night by singing *I Am Who I Am*, followed by taking off her wig.

Yes... I'm not kidding. Welcome to show business!

We would do our run of shows, and after the finale on Sunday evening, all we wanted to do is drive home. Phyllis took her sweet time paying us, sometimes making us wait an hour or two to get paid for no reason whatsoever.

To this day, I'm very conscientious when it comes to finances. If I owe anyone, I never want that person to have to ask for their money. I also make sure that my contract stipulates that I will never have to ask for my check.

All because of Phyllis.

The here-and-there gigs didn't pay a whole lot, so to make extra money, I started teaching traffic school. There was an ad in *Variety* that read, "Comedians Wanted." I called the number and signed up to be a traffic school instructor. The name of the company that ran it was called Lettuce Amuse U.

Cute, huh? Okay, maybe not.

The irony that I had a shitty driving record and had to spend my own fair share of time at traffic school was not lost on me. It should have worried me that it didn't seem to bother the owners of the school, who were a sight to behold. He looked like a scared white rabbit, and his wife looked like Gladys Kravitz from *Bewitched*.

The second one.

The more I taught the class, the more successful I became as a comedian, and the more notoriety I was attracting. News people wanted to interview me, and television and print were calling, too. Justine Bateman took the class, and was so sweet to me by helping me get cast in a bit-part for a TV movie she starred in called *Can You Feel Me Dancing*? It was my ninth acting job ever, but only the fifth one that paid. And playing her brother was her real brother Jason Bateman!

I became the most sought after traffic school teacher in the school, which both thrilled and pissed off the owners at the same time.

It also got me on my first talk show, a tiny little program called *The Merv Griffin Show*. I was absolutely stunned at my good fortune. The booker of Merv's show asked me to come to his office and had me do my set as a preview for the show. So I came, I saw, I conquered. He loved the set and he said I had the show. Just like that.

And not only was I going to get to do my act, but I would also get a place on the couch, afterwards, and it was in the planning of the couch where Merv showed me just how good he was at what he did. He said that when I was in the middle of a string of jokes, to touch his hand while he was leaning in so that he would know not to interrupt my flow.

What a pro!

On that first appearance, I wore a tiger jacket, and my first joke was, "Every time I wear this jacket, I feel like saying, 'Wilma, let me in!' I think she was just mad because she had one big boob."

The audience roared. I know I would have been back had the program stayed on the air. Just three months later, the legend retired his popular show.

But doing that episode brought me to another member of talk show royalty: Ed McMahon and *Star Search*. I'd only been a comedian for three years when I got that break. I was still in my comedic infancy, but I still somehow managed to pull off a win on my first appearance.

However, a burgeoning young comedian named Martin Lawrence knocked me out of the competition the next week, winning by three-quarters of a point.

Damn, Gina!

So to be funny, I stomped my foot and walked off, throwing my head back as I sauntered out. At the time, it was received incredibly well. People totally got the joke. But as the years went on, and clips were shown on the Internet... well...

... wow... people sure do have a lot of opinions. I went from being cool and hip to "who the fuck does he think he is?" in the blink of an eye and the click of a mouse.

My career continued its ascent, this time on an airplane. My first job outside of California was opening for Shirley Hemphill from the hit TV show *What's Happening!!...* in Oklahoma City. She hit the stage and the audience went absolutely bonkers as she said her catchphrase, "What's

Happening!!" It was at that moment when I realized just what the power of fame meant.

Shirley taught me a lot on that trip. For instance, she got half of her money up front, and the other half the day she arrived... in cash. Her reason was that a lot of times you worked for people you'd never met, and you didn't know if you could trust them to pay you. And it really wasn't a big deal. Many bookers were originally bar owners who went into the comedy business. They knew the workings of an all-cash transaction.

Shirley was from a small town in North Carolina. Her show was about her journey from being dirt poor to becoming a major television star, and they loved her.

I had never hung out with somebody that famous before. She asked me and the featured act, Vince Champ, to go see the new Richard Gere film, *King David*. Vince and I laughed through the entire movie because it was so bad. Being a religious woman, Shirley was so upset that she didn't speak with us until the next day.

She opened the door to the possibility of us conversing again with this little gem: "Jason, you're a good dresser, what do you think of my outfit? Does it make me look like a lesbian?"

Keep in mind that both of us were still in the closet then. She wore a pair of men's running pants with a stripe down the side, a fitted button-down oxford shirt, diamond stud earrings, and very white tennis shoes.

I simply said, "Yes, Shirl," and she, again, gave me the twenty-four hour silent treatment.

After that, we became fast friends, and she was always so kind to me when we would run into each other at The Comedy Store or The Laugh Factory.

Now Vince Champ was another story... a story that would get him incarcerated...

... for a looooooong time.

Vince was the first comedian who really helped me get road gigs. He lived in LA in a bachelor apartment, and he would always call and ask me to go have chow with him when he was not on tour, which was not very often. He traveled a lot. He was a tall, handsome man who was known to have a very generic stand-up comedy act.

In fact, other comedians referred to him as "The Game Show Host" due to his innate ability to not tick off a crowd. But he was funny… that was undeniable.

During our lunches, he gave me information on which stand-up bookers to call for gigs, and the wisdom on how to handle them. He would give me road contacts, and I would give him TV contacts… including an opening for his own appearance on *Star Search*.

Years later, much to my unbridled shock, Vince was arrested and convicted for being a serial rapist.

I'm not kidding.

He's still in jail to this day for raping women on college campuses. I never saw it coming… and I'm still gobsmacked. I guess it's true when they say you really can't judge a book by its cover.

I became a very successful feature act in the Funny Bone comedy club circuit around the country. As the middle act of the night, I could earn almost eight or nine hundred dollars a week, plus airfare. They'd even put me up in a hotel, or give me a room in their comedy condo. Working on the road and finally being able to do six to eight shows a week made me realize that I was not a prisoner of my last set. Just because the eight o'clock show may not have been great didn't mean the ten-thirty show could not be amazing.

Unless it was a Friday. Second shows on Friday are always the worst shows of the week. Most of the audience had been up since seven a.m., worked a full day, and choked down enough liquor to flatten a mule. You do the math.

Once, I got a job as an opening act in Amarillo, Texas, and this is really where I started to learn that I was… how do I put this… not like everyone else.

This show's gonna be juuuuust a little bit different.

I opened up for this really funny southern comedian whose name I forget, and to be honest, my sets were not going great. My saving grace was that the owner's wife loved me. In those days, I would wear a different outfit every night, and I prided myself on my originality. I was still relatively new at this, but whatever I lacked in material, I more than made up for with my quick wit and my repartee with the audience.

Now keep in mind, I was still in the closet in those days, and had no way of protecting myself... in Amarillo, Texas.

After my second show one night, I got a call from the club owner, and in the nicest way he said, "Ima hafta let you go."

"Why?" I asked. "I know I'm not doing great, but it's still early in the week."

"I think you're doin' fine, boy," he said, "but there's some people here in this town that wanna kill you."

He told me he would pay me my full salary, which was incredibly generous of him. Out of that, I paid fifty dollars to change my plane ticket and I went home with my tail between my legs. For the first time, I fully realized the uphill battle I would have to wage.

Once when I was in St. Louis, Missouri, I was asked by a local booker if I would mind replacing another comedian at a college for a lunch show.

"Of course, I'd love to! I'm free during the day. Thank you for thinking of me!" I think it's always important to show gratitude.

The show was in a common space at the college. For those of you who don't know, a common space is a large hall-like room, with doors to classrooms all around you, and an exit at each end. In the middle of the room was a riser with a microphone stand on top. There were chairs laid out in rows on one side of the temporary stage.

The problem was that there was no back to the stage. So in theory, if someone didn't like my act, or the fact that I was gay, and they wanted to do something about it, I would have no warning or defense at all. And at this particular gig, I was not promoted; I was the replacement for another comedian. So because these kids didn't know who they were getting, and because it was at a college in the 90's, the odds were stronger than usual that this show might go south.

To that young college student producing the event, I looked like a total diva. At first, I refused to go on. Then there were phone calls made, and then more calls made, and in the midst of it all, I was having a full-blown panic attack. At the time, I didn't have the tools to communicate what I was really feeling, nor did I even know. It felt like what I thought a nervous breakdown might feel like.

Ten years later in a therapy session, I was told that at that moment, I was having a post-traumatic stress episode from the way I was treated when I went to school. When coupled with the many times as a comedian that I had been heckled, or catcalled, or threatened with potential violence, it was a recipe for potential disaster.

I remember hanging up the phone with the booker… who I thought probably would never hire me again… and making the decision to go back down, bite the bullet, and do my show.

Thankfully, it was much ado about nothing. In fact, I remember it was an unusually good show. But I learned something about myself that I needed to overcome. I needed to own my history, to acknowledge it, and to move past it. These were the things that I had to do to take back my life as a human being… and I didn't quite realize that I had the power to do it.

Yet.

Years later, after I became a successful headliner in mainstream comedy clubs, and doing so by being one of the first openly gay comedians to sell out all over the country, the same booker from the college common room gig booked me at his club in Des Moines, Iowa. The shows were going extremely well; I was killing it. But there was a problem that occurred every night. The club would only pick me up about fifteen minutes before my act.

The opener went from eight to eight-twenty. The feature would take it until eight-forty-five, and then I would go on until nine-thirty.

I used to like to watch the audience for a short while before my set so that I could gauge the tone of the room, but I was not given the opportunity or the respect to have my fairly miniscule needs met.

This went on for the first three days of a five-day gig. On night four, I called the club and asked why I wasn't getting picked up when the show started, and the club owner screamed, "I'll pick you up when I'm goddamn good and ready!" And then he hung up on me.

When the car eventually arrived and I showed up to the club, I saw him when I walked into the bar area. This couldn't go on. So I went over and stood up for myself, asking why he wouldn't afford me the courtesy of being picked up a little earlier.

"Get out of here," he smirked.

So I did what I always did: I went on stage and tore it up with the crowd, earning a standing ovation. And then two hours later, I did it again.

I went back to my hotel, feeling quite satisfied with myself.

The next night, which was the last night of the gig, I was picked up and brought to the club. There was a sign saying that the final night had been cancelled. The owner gave me my check, pro-rated to not include the last night, breaking my contract. He then grabbed my arm, walked me out of the club, and said, "You're fired."

And just to add insult to injury, there was a police officer friend of his standing outside of the club... watching. It was a deeply humiliating experience. Of course, the owner made sure no one drove me back to my hotel. Thankfully, one of the waitresses took pity on the situation and gave me a ride back.

Welcome to the Midwest! My only experience with Middle America included Andy Griffith and Barney Fife. Mayberry, this was not.

If clicking my heels three times together could have gotten me back to Los Angeles in that instant, I would have channeled my inner Judy Garland on the spot.

Oy!

Touring the country as an openly gay comedian was a real education for me. Because of my family and living in Los Angeles, I had very few experiences with people who either weren't in show business or New York Jews.

I used to work eight shows a week whenever I'd visit The Punchline comedy club in Columbia, South Carolina. Sometimes, when I headlined The Funny Bone in St. Louis, I would do ten shows a week because I was doing so well selling tickets.

The problem was that I never really got what I like to call "straight-boy money." I always had to fight to get paid equally. Now one of the dirty little secrets about the comedy circuit is that not all comics are treated the same. In fact, women and minorities… myself included in this category… are often not paid equally, and the rationale is that it's assumed we would sell fewer tickets than our white male Christian heterosexual counterparts. Club owners believed that the audience would not "get us."

But the truth is that I held my own, and I worked hard as a comedian, and as a promoter of my own shows. As a comic, you have to do three things really well. First, you have to be funny. Next, you have to do the time… anywhere from forty-five minutes to an hour. And lastly, you have to be able to sell tickets.

So with each new city, I would hit the ground running. I would get myself featured in an article in the local newspaper. I would get a pic of the week in the local entertainment magazines, and I would get the cover of the local gay rag.

Then, I would contact the local affiliate of one of the network TV shows that I had been on, i.e. ABC for *The Drew Carey Show*.

But the big draw for my audience was radio. I would go to as many radio shows as would have me, and my trick was to stay on as long as I could. I knew that the longer I was featured, the more people would come to the show. And if they tried to say goodbye to me, I would start to tell another story about a celebrity that the hosts loved, or I would flirt with somebody on the air, which would usually get me an extra segment or two.

The audience loved it, and my shows sold out.

But as you can see, it's quite the workload. It was so heavy that I couldn't enjoy much of the success that I achieved. And the pressure that I put on myself to chase that success was enormous. I was always terrified of making a mistake for fear of not being asked back, so I did everything I could think of to make sure that that didn't happen.

In those days, there was no Internet to get your face in front of perspective audience members, so I would have posters made and send them in a mailing tube to the club. I had hoped that the club owners would have the good sense to use these free marketing materials to attract a fuller house, but I would often see the mailing tube in the office of the club owner, unopened.

Once in South Bend, Indiana, I asked why the owner didn't take any posters to the local gay bar to share before the shows. This three-hundred-fifty-pound club owner named Bart said, "I'm sorry, I can't go into a gay bar. What would I do if someone tried to pick me up?"

I wanted to say, "You're like a piece of furniture. Someone picking you up is most likely never going to happen."

Of course, this was before the "Bear" culture was en vogue. He might have had his chance if he'd just waited a bit longer.

Another time, I was headlining The Punchline in Greenville, South Carolina. I was having a great time, and the audience was exceptionally diverse... a veritable color-wheel of people. On Friday night between the first and second show, a waitress used the N-word describing some of my African American fans... thinking that I would somehow be complicit with this racist comment.

Let me make this perfectly clear: I was not about to be complicit. I told her in no way, shape, or form that she was to speak that way around me.

"Well why?" she asked. "They're not here, they can't hear you."

"It doesn't matter," I said. "I don't use that word. And I'd prefer if you don't use it around me."

Actually, she never used any words around me ever again, which was fine.

The Holy Grail that every openly gay comedian wants to capture is to headline their own show in Provincetown, Massachusetts. It's like the gay Mecca of vacations. My stand-up agent, Shelly Weiss with OUTmedia, got me a gig to headline Tropical Joe's, a local restaurant and cabaret just one block off the strip.

They had the best coconut shrimp I've ever eaten, by the way.

I was booked for the eight o'clock show, with the ten being headlined by the drag-a-pella Beauty Shop Quartet called The Kinsey Sicks. I was releasing my first comedy CD called *Gay Comedy Without a Dress*, and I really wanted to make the most of this opportunity.

In your contract for Provincetown, you were required to hand out fliers on the street for at least three hours a day, which was brutal... even more so when the playing field is stacked against you. A drag queen can wear a gorgeous dress and platform shoes and attract attention. *Naked Boys Singing* could walk around in their towels and sell tickets right on the street. But your run-of-the-mill funny gay Jewish comedian, whose show was described as outrageous and quick witted in the comedy clubs, was thought to be rude and inappropriate on the streets of P-town.

It was shocking to me how difficult it was to get my gay brothers to come see my show. Yet at the same time, many wanted pictures with me and autographs. Everything was copasetic with us, as long as I would not try to compete with Cher, Barbra, Liza, or *Naked Boys Singing*.

Still, when people came to the show, we had the best time ever. But getting them there was like pulling teeth. I'd never had to work so hard to attract an audience. Yet on the other side of the coin, when I would perform for Gay Prides, gay political events, AIDS benefits, and working with the Human Rights Campaign... gay men would come in droves, and the shows were always outrageously fun.

Thankfully, much of my career could be described in the same way: outrageously fun. I have had the privilege to work with an astonishing amount of the funniest people in the world, including Lea DeLaria... the first gay woman on *The Arsenio Hall Show.*

Lea scares the shit out of me, in a good way. One year, I was in a car in the West Hollywood Gay Pride Parade. There was a sign on the car door that read Jason Stuart, Comedy Central's *Out There In Hollywood.* As I was waiting for my turn to enter the parade, Lea walked by and yelled, "What took you so long? Why didn't you come out years ago?"

I took a beat and I said, "I didn't know I could."

I don't think she realized what an impact coming out made on me. She always had the courage to be out, and unapologetically herself, from the word go. It took me a bit longer.

I want to take a moment to say that almost all the comedians who I have worked with have given me the career that I have today, whether it be influencing me through their work, giving me a job, or simply talking me down from a bad set. And so many of these comedians never hesitated to tell me when I did well, or if they had a tag for a bit that I was working on.

"Thank you" will never, ever, be enough.

# 10

## To All the Men I've Loved Before

When I was a child, Alan was my first love. In fact, he's one of my earliest memories. I actually don't remember a day in my life when I didn't know him. When we would ride bikes or have sleepovers, all was right with the world. Of course, there was nothing sexual as we were both so young, but I knew that I was at my happiest whenever I was around him. Deep down as I look back, I know he was my first inkling that I was homosexual, though I didn't know what the word meant. I just knew that being gay was bad because that's all I ever heard from people. I knew they were feelings that I better keep to myself.

Alan moved away sometime before junior high school. It was only about fifteen miles away in an area called Beverly Glen. It was a new housing project on the wrong side of the tracks of Bel Air, but it might as well have been across the country. We visited a few times, but it wasn't the same. And since he wasn't gay, we didn't share the same feelings... no matter how much I wanted them reciprocated. And if Alan wasn't going to be gay, then I would probably never be gay, either.

Like it was my choice. Oy!

As I entered junior high school, I tried really hard to get a girlfriend. It was like my job. The first girl I ever French-kissed was named Michelle. We were both set up on a date by our mutual friends Brad and Annette who were already a couple... a couple who I set up!

What can I say? The matchmaker Dolly Levi in *Hello, Dolly!* made a big impression on me! Thank you, Barbra.

Michelle and I could not have been more mismatched. It felt like someone was trying to squeeze me into a pair of skinny jeans that would never fit; buttoning the waist is one thing, but navigating the zipper is quite another.

Not being heterosexual didn't come from a lack of trying on my part. I lost my virginity to a girl named Carol. I took her to a cheap motel on La Cienega Boulevard, where I tried my best to… um… perform. I could barely get it in because I couldn't get it up. It was pure devastation on every level. That day, I truly knew that I'd never play with the other team no matter how much I liked the outfits, which was a lot.

I don't know how you straight people do it!

When I moved out at eighteen, by hook or by crook, I was determined to be a heterosexual. So for six months, I stopped any pursuit of anonymous sex with men. In those days, anonymity was the only game in town. There was no Grindr, Scruff, or anything-dot-com. No AOL chat rooms. No place to meet if you were gay, unless you were willing to out yourself by walking into a gay bar. For one thing, I was not old enough, but the real reason for my watering hole abstinence was over the fear of losing my burgeoning acting career. So I kept things on the down-low.

When I was in my early twenties, I met a banker named Frank, who I told my family and friends was named Francis. I met him for the first time at a bath house on Lankershim Boulevard in North Hollywood.

On the surface, these were places open to the public where you could work out and go for a steam bath afterwards. The workout facilities weren't really of the Gold's Gym caliber; they'd maybe have an exercise bike, a dumbbell or two, and not much else.

Beneath the surface, these were also places where gay men would go to meet, work out, enjoy a steam bath, and have anonymous sex, which… truth be told… was the selling point. They would have these little rooms where you could go to "rest," though not much resting was accomplished.

There's a book called *Gay New York* by George Chauncey that talks about the origin of the bath house, at least in that part of the country. In those days, you had to be affluent to have an actual bath for washing in your home. Instead, people did what my mother called "the TPA: tit's, pit's and ass" with a pitcher of water, a wash cloth, and a bowl on a daily basis. They would save the luxury of a bath as a once-a-week treat. And since the bath houses were segregated by gender, and you had a bunch of naked men in close proximity to each other...

... let the games begin!

When I saw Frank for the first time, our eyes locked. Each of us wore nothing but a towel and a smile. He was a few years older than me, and he looked like a Jewish Burt Reynolds... dark, with a thick mustache. We met near the hot tub, and he was the first man who ever treated me like a human being and not a sex object. He was smart, worldly, compassionate, and well put-together.

After that first afternoon, Frank pursued me. I'd never had anyone do that before, and it made me completely uncomfortable and excited at the same time. Agreeing to something deeper with Frank would have hastened me coming out of the closet, which I could not see the possibility of doing.

He had an apartment with two bedrooms... one on each side with a living room in the middle. He lived there with his boyfriend of many years, but the way the apartment was set up enabled them to give the impression to anyone who came over that they were nothing but platonic roommates. How crazy is that to have to go to that extent?

Plus, who did they think they were kidding? They both had their "own bedroom." Not gay? I don't think so!

Some mornings, Frank would come to my house before work and sleep with me in my Murphy bed for a half-hour before heading to the office. He would put mix-tapes together for me of music that he loved. He took me on business trips with him, and while he was in meetings, I would go to the movies during the day and make love with him at night. No one had ever treated me so kindly. He made me feel like I mattered.

He even talked about leaving his boyfriend, which frightened me… not because I felt remorse over being a final catalyst of a broken relationship, but because I was not out of the closet and could not see how it would work. It was only 1980 and I was so young. I simply wasn't ready for what it all meant.

Many years later, a friend asked me if I felt at all guilty about being "the other woman" in that relationship. My mother had an affair with the butcher for fifteen years of a twenty-two-year marriage. My uncle had sex with anything that moved. I didn't really have role models in the monogamy department. But honestly, there was a thin layer of guilt in the back of my mind.

And just the idea that I could have a relationship with a man seemed so foreign to me; I could not grasp the concept. And besides, seeing as how Frank was already in a serious relationship, it afforded me the luxury of staying in the closet. The status quo was just fine with me… for a while.

But eventually, my feelings would betray me: I was slowly and irreversibly falling in love with him.

One night, we went to dinner at this little Italian restaurant near my one-room apartment. He always knew where the best restaurants were. After the meal, we took a walk and he started to talk to me about the possibility of me coming out in my life… not even in my work, but just my life. I cried harder than I've ever cried because it totally hit me that I was gay, and there was no going back. He held me and got me through it.

He wanted to take the relationship further, but I couldn't bring myself to do it. Frustrated with the situation, I broke it off shortly after that. I was twenty-one and lost.

A year later when I moved into my new one-bedroom apartment with terra cotta walls, I called him and asked him if he ever really loved me. He said, "It was so long ago, I don't remember." I was so terribly hurt by him for saying that. To this day, I don't know if he meant it, or if he was protecting himself. And sadly, I'll never know. I hope it was the latter.

As I was writing this book, I discovered that Frank died in 2008. He was just 57.

After that fateful day at the bath house, I don't actually remember ever going back there to meet anyone else, but it didn't matter. Thankfully, they weren't the only places to anonymously meet men. You could go to certain parks, and even bathrooms at various department stores across the country.

Yes, seriously.

The general public didn't know what was going on, but the signs were evident if you knew what to look for. A lot of times, you could see gay men silently communicating with each other. After a while and a bit of experience, I got really good at being able to find cruising spots almost anywhere I traveled in the country.

I know it might sound sleazy at first, but there was a certain excitement finding the opportunities to explore my fledgling sexuality. I had so little experience, and this was my baptism by fire. It was dangerous and thrilling, and I can't even begin to tell you some of the things that went on.

Okay, maybe a few things.

Once, I was standing at a urinal at a West Hollywood park, and a guy the spitting image of Pat Morita from *The Karate Kid* walked right up to me. I looked away because I was uninterested, embarrassed, and because I was busy actually peeing. There were half-walls separating the urinals, so they would have provided a modicum of privacy for any other people in the bathroom who might have been interested in doing things if Arnold from *Happy Days* hadn't shown up. There was literally nothing going on, but that wasn't good enough for Mr. Myagi. We were gay, and our potentially illicit thoughts were enough for him to whip out a badge and arrest everyone in the bathroom, to my absolute horror.

My dad came to bail me out; I told him that it was a case of entrapment, which it kind of was. Lenny wasn't having it… he was quite pissed, but at least he got me out of there. I could not say the same for my cell mate, who was also arrested by Myagi-san. I felt bad for the guy because no one came to pick him up. He was probably close to fifty, and I doubt his wife was in any hurry to get him out of there. It's pretty depressing to think about the whole fiasco.

Thank God times have changed where we don't have to live underground anymore. Of course, that presents its own set of challenges. Now we have the ease of meeting on apps. But you can never tell when a conversation is over because it never really is. No one says "goodbye" or "talk to you later" or "I have a call" or "I'm busy, but I like you." It may be more open, but it can also be more confusing!

There was nothing confusing about being arrested for sex in a public place. I thought I was in a serious mess. I learned quickly that it was nothing that a few shekels couldn't fix. In those days when you got in trouble, you could find a lawyer in the advertising section of the gay rags. I found a lesbian attorney who charged five hundred bucks to go to court for me to make it go away. She got a cut, as I'm sure others did, too. It seemed like a purely money-making venture, but it worked. My mom called me shortly after agreeing to pay half the ransom, with my dad paying the other half. She said she didn't want to do it, and she became very angry with me about being gay… so angry, in fact, that she rescinded her half of the payment… leaving my father with the entire bill.

And then, the hammer fell.

"How can you be involved with that kind of sex?" she snapped.

To her, this was evidential proof that I was gay; it had finally sunk in, and she really didn't know how to handle it. At that moment, I couldn't necessarily blame her. But in the next instant, she hung up on me, and I had had it. I immediately called her back and said, "If you hang up on me again, I won't be calling you back."

*click*

I was devastated, but I knew that I needed to stand up for myself and stay true to my word. Most of my childhood, my mother would get angry at me for something and I would apologize. That unspoken agreement needed to stop. It was hard to let it go, but also liberating in a way.

Nine months after that fateful phone call, I was downtown at Castle Neckwear, my father's necktie manufacturing company. I sat in his office, waiting for him to get off the phone so that we could have lunch. He was talking to my mother to discuss a problem that she was having with my sister, again. My father knew what had happened between us, and he had been trying to get us back together. So he told my mother that I was in his office and that she and I should talk. He then handed me the phone, and that first conversation was the beginning of our recovery as mother and son. It was awkward, but it was a start.

Whenever I look back upon this chapter in my life, it always surprises me that I had the self-esteem to detach from my mom for a short while. It taught me to let her opinion of me go. I was able to live my life for no one but me, and that's a pretty powerful thing. It still took me years to let go of the shame of getting caught.

And I wasn't even having sex! Well, that time…

But the good thing is my mother and I have not only repaired our relationship but it has grown deeper and more connected as the years go by. She has changed and become the most important person in my life. Forgiveness is a gift. Remember that.

In Los Angeles off Melrose, there used to be a place where you could cruise in your car and meet gay men after dark. I even saw a couple of famous guys who I won't mention, but Robert Reed, the dad from *The Brady Bunch* was one of them. Of course he was past his prime, but that didn't matter to me.

Oh the fantasies I had about him catching me and Christopher Knight, "Peter," in his den. Maybe he would discipline us. And then again, maybe he wouldn't. Also keep in mind that "Peter" and I were both teenagers at the time. These are old fantasies!

It seemed very apropos for Los Angeles to have a place like this, as this is the antithesis of a walking city. We all practically live in our cars. At the cruising spot, you drive around until you see a guy you like, sometimes passing each other three or four times until you work up the courage to make your move. Then you wave him over, you both park off to the side, and you talk.

And this is where I met Barry Robins.

He was almost exactly fourteen years older than me... our birthdays separated by a day (his January 12, mine the 13th). He was on the short side, and he looked young for his age. He had dark hair and a moustache like Burt Reynolds (are you seeing a pattern here?), and he drove an old beat-up Buick, but that made no difference to me.

I fell in love with him after the first time I went back to his apartment. He had album covers all over his walls near the ceiling, and they were all opera singers, including Leontyne Price, Maria Callas, and more I can't even remember.

He had been a successful actor, studying with the legendary Stella Adler. He even starred in a film I loved called *Bless the Beasts and Children*, directed by Stanley Kramer, though I hadn't realized it at the time of our first meeting. He had guest-starred on *Columbo*, *The Girl from U.N.C.L.E.*, and even played the crown prince in *The King and I* at Lincoln Center in New York, continuing in the role while touring all over the country. He became a mentor of sorts to me; I was Eliza Doolittle to his Henry Higgins. He introduced me to different artists and the theatre and things that I had yet to experience.

I think he played the line of being in and out of the closet. All his friends knew, but the general public didn't, which was pretty common for those days. It certainly wasn't an issue in the theatre, but it was in the film and TV world. Another strike was that he looked very young and boyish for his age, and his height could be described as vertically challenged. I think there were so many things stacked against him, and he was unable to duplicate his early magic and make a living as an actor.

Instead, he tended bar at a lesbian establishment on Pico Boulevard in West LA which did not help his situation. He was desperately unhappy, forced to take jobs that he really didn't want to do just to survive. Disenchanted with bar life, he eventually became a masseur… catering to the general public and at least one very famous actor would come out a year later. Rock Hudson.

Barry and I were inseparable. I had never been around someone who was so cultured and worldly, and I could not get enough of our time together. He meant everything to me.

Our relationship was never consummated, but he did kiss me and even once took a bath with me, which was incredibly romantic. For a while, I wondered why he didn't want to take things further physically, but soon I learned the truth: Barry had an unknown disease, and his condition was getting worse.

He went to the doctor for some unusual symptoms that he had been experiencing, but they couldn't give him a diagnosis… a diagnosis that turned out to be HIV. I think he knew, somehow, what he had, and he didn't want me to befall the same fate. So he would playfully rebuff me, telling me that I was too young or not his type, even though he would constantly ask me to come over. He knew that we couldn't be fully intimate with each other, but I believe that our time together meant as much to him as it did to me.

When he became wracked with full-blown AIDS, he stopped returning my calls. He also wouldn't answer the door when I would stop by. Yes, dropping by unannounced used to be a thing. It devastated me that he completely shut me out.

I phoned his mother several times, and she finally answered. She told me that he died. I felt like my entire world had stopped; my heart missed a beat, and I couldn't catch my breath. I never got the chance to spend another day with him, or to even say goodbye. It also gives me chills knowing I'm now older than he ever lived.

Barry's death in 1986 changed me. HIV and AIDS were now in the full consciousness of almost everyone around the world, thanks in large part to the revelation made by Rock Hudson that he was in the grips of the disease. It was a stunning admission not only of his illness, but also his homosexuality. He was the first truly high-profile person with full-blown AIDS to come forward, and because of his friendship with Elizabeth Taylor, she was able to start raising money for research that eventually led to a treatment for this illness that was once considered a death sentence. So many people are alive today, in part, because of that first push to try and find a cure.

And with that research came the knowledge that this was not some smite from any deity. At first, it was referred to as the gay plague, and it felt like it: this was a disease that, on the surface, targeted gay men and killed virtually everyone it infected. If you remember, AIDS – Acquired Immune Deficiency Syndrome, was originally called GRID – Gay Related Immune Deficiency.

It seemed like the only people who were on our side at that time were lesbians… and I'm not sure I personally know a lesbian who has gotten the disease. It didn't matter to them: they stood with their gay brothers, and it made a huge difference. That fact touches my heart in a big way.

As it turned out, it was a disease that was transmitted by blood and blood products. Unprotected sex without condoms, high-risk intravenous drug use, and even blood transfusions could all be catalysts.

Like it did for many others, AIDS changed the way I thought about my future, the way I had sex, and how I saw myself. It was a constant reminder of mortality… something that most people only start to think about in their sixties and seventies, not in their mid-twenties. *Entertainment Weekly* used to put out a list every year of famous people who died of AIDS; I always knew more people on the list than I wanted to.

And now Barry was one of them. I regret that I didn't sit by his door until he answered it. I regret that I didn't try harder. I still miss him to this day, and I always will. It's not an excuse, but I was just so young and unprepared to deal with that kind of situation.

One time at a different cruising spot, I met Alejandro Rey while driving on Sunset Boulevard in West Hollywood. He was in a convertible; I was in my Toyota Tercel... a car that I had bought with the money I made playing a dishwasher in a Red Lobster commercial.

As we passed each other the first time, I thought, 'Hey, that looks like Carlos from *The Flying Nun!*'

After a few more passes, he motioned for me to hang a left so that we could park and talk. As I got out of the car, I confirmed that he was indeed Carlos from *The Flying Nun.*

"Hello," he said in a thick Latin accent. "My name is Alejandro."

"Hi Ah-le-HAND-ro," I smiled slyly.

"No, it's Ah-le-HAWN-dro," he said, irritated, which made the whole scene even funnier.

We exchanged numbers which started a year-long affair. He was always very tough on me about my acting career, saying that I did everything wrong, which I never appreciated. So I continued to mispronounce his name, which he never appreciated. In the least.

We hung out whenever he wanted to, which was fine with me; I wasn't looking for anything too serious after Frank. He taught me to play chess, though I had to be naked whenever we played. The relationship eventually petered away, which made me sad... though I can't say I missed his bossiness.

He died of cancer in 1987 at the age of 57. Years later, a feature story was being done on me by Lydia Marcus for *Frontiers Magazine* because of a film I was in titled *Coffee Date*, which also starred Wilson Cruz, Sally Kirkland, Jonathan Silverman, and... yes... Debbie Gibson. During the interview, she asked me if I ever had sex with anyone famous.

"Yes, I had an affair with Alejandro Rey," I replied nonchalantly. It was a miniscule part of a nice long interview, and I never thought anything of it since he had passed away several years prior. It was a blip on my radar that didn't even register.

The next thing I know, a burgeoning gossip columnist named Perez Hilton picked up the story and ran with it. On his website chat room, someone commented, "Who the hell does Jason Stuart think he is, bragging that he had sex with Alejandro Rey?"

Someone else replied, "Who the fuck is Alejandro Rey?"

And I thought to myself, 'Oh my God, I've arrived!'

A month later, my three-line mention of Alejandro turned into a full-blown article in the *National Enquirer* with the headline, "*Flying Nun's* Star's Secret Gay Life Revealed!"

A few years later, I was at the Sundance Film Festival for the first time. Dave Annable, who starred in *Brothers & Sisters* with Sally Field, informed me that someone told Sally about the *Enquirer* piece, and she seemed surprised. She laughed and said she had no idea. She, herself, has a gay son of whom she's very supportive, and she thought she might have seen the signs, but she hadn't.

So it became a full gay Hollywood circle!

I got my first gig in Vegas in a restaurant/bar in 1990, and I was over the moon. Sure, it wasn't at Caesars Palace or even Circus Circus, but it was a big deal. It was only one night, but that was enough for me. I thought it would be one of the bigger steps in my comedy and acting future, but like so many things in Vegas, what you see is not always what you get.

I was still in the closet at that point in my work, often wrestling with the potential consequences to my career, but I was out in my private life. While it sounds impossible to live this way, it wasn't difficult for me to compartmentalize things… I'd done it for as long as I could remember, and in many cases, keeping things separate was simply more familiar to me at the time.

Vegas certainly wasn't about meeting a boyfriend; it was solely about my work, and I was laser-focused. I would do my show, make people laugh, and maybe get noticed by an agent looking for new talent to act in a sitcom pilot where I could play the funny neighbor. That was my dream at the time. I had no idea just how much things were about to be thrown into utter chaos.

The show went well. It was packed, and the crowd seemed to love me. After the set, I saw a man across the crowded room. He looked like a young Howard Rollins Jr. from *Ragtime*, and he took my breath away. Much like Cher described meeting Sonny for the first time, "there was this glow around him."

He had this incredible smile and beautiful big brown eyes, and I was drawn to him like a moth to a flame. The way he moved and interacted with those around him was magnetic. I fell big for him.

I walked over to him, and we talked. His name was Tony, and he was more beautiful than I could have imagined. He said he worked with the band Shalamar, and had co-written *The Power* by a group called Snap! He said all the right things, and I was enamored as well as impressed. As I gave him my number, he told me that he wanted to help me in my career. This was the beginning of our relationship.

He lived with a woman who had several children, though they weren't married; in fact, he said the relationship was ending. I later found out that the children weren't actually his. He, himself, was divorced from a drug addict… so the story goes. They had a child together, Raymond.

He would call me, or even just show up unannounced. We would drive down the coast to San Diego to visit a friend, or we would sometimes go to clubs… but only straight clubs. He would never refer to me as his date, which completely confused me. He would introduce me as the comedian from *Star Search* who lost to Martin Lawrence.

Whenever we were alone, he was incredibly flirtatious, saying that he had never had these kind of feelings for a man the way he had for me. He called me his boyfriend, and we talked of having a future together. To punctuate it, he would even say, "I mean it, baby."

When we were in public?

"Hi, this is Jason… my friend."

He always had some crazy scheme going on, too… how to get rich quick or pull off this legitimately unbelievable deal here or there. And eventually, when things would go south, his feelings of confident success transformed into those of abject failure, and there was never anything in between. He simply could not seem to move forward from the wreckage of his past.

Yet for some insane reason, I loved being around him. Maybe it was because he made me feel like I was the only person on earth whenever we were alone. Of course, maybe it was because compared to his, my life was the picture of tranquility. It's quite the balancing act of trying to date a human roller coaster.

I remember our first kiss. It sent electricity throughout my body like I'd never felt. But after a while, that feeling faded and I realized that his kiss wasn't enough; our relationship was going nowhere. In my mind, I thought that we might as well have already been broken up, so I asked him to stop calling me.

For a while I didn't hear from him, but then one day he called to tell me he was leaving his girlfriend, and that he wanted to consummate our relationship. It sounded so convincing, but like so many things with him, they were just words; it didn't happen, so I refused to see him.

About a year after that fateful night in Vegas, I got a collect call from the Chino State Penitentiary. It was Tony. He told me that he had gotten a job delivering packages to people, and was now caught up in some sort of drug ring.

Now keep in mind that Tony was incredibly fit and health conscious and never did any drugs, himself, so it was quite a shock that he would have had anything to do with them at all.

He continued to call me from prison professing his love for me, saying that because he had time to think, he realized he couldn't handle his feelings for me before, but now he could. And with that, he had me:

hook, line, and prison. I sent him a little money. I sent him clothes. I supported him emotionally in the best way that I could.

After a year and a half behind bars, he was released from prison. He came back to my house where we made love for the first time. It was explosive in literally every way imaginable. Up until that moment, I had never had such strong emotional and physical feelings for anyone or anything in my life. I didn't know they were possible.

He stayed with me for a while until I helped him find an apartment and a job; things were looking up. Sadly, things would be looking down soon enough as his façade began to crumble. He couldn't seem to stay employed, and his behavior veered into the manic as some of his perceived successes gave way to his actual failures; he took himself to some very dark places that I was not prepared for.

As our time together progressed, Tony talked me into buying him things. He always had an answer for any question I had, and he always swore to pay me back. Once, I had gotten a gig in Sacramento, and he said he wanted to come with me so that he could see his ex-girlfriend with whom he had a kid.

Excuse me? He had another kid?

What?!

Unsurprisingly, this was news to me. He also insisted that we rent a Cadillac instead of driving my Toyota Tercel up to the show. So we picked it up.

Yes, we picked it up. Can you believe I did this?

He tore off the rental car sticker, presumably so that he could tell his ex that this was his car and that he was doing very well for himself.

On the way up, he then told me that he had hidden fifty thousand dollars that he nicked from the drug dealers in an old tire in his ex-girlfriend's garage, and that he would be able to pay back all the money that he owed me and we could finally start our life together. He even said that his older son, Raymond, would come to live with us as his mother was unable to take care of him, which made me so sad.

Of course, I was blinded by love, so I went along with everything. I was too young and too naïve to know any better.

I did my show that night, and then the next day, he took the car to see his ex and their son, and to grab the money from the tire. Hours later, when he finally got back, he told me that the money wasn't there, and that she had apparently put it in a storage bin in Los Angeles.

When we got back to my apartment in LA, he finally told me the truth: there was no money. I can't say that I was blindsided by the revelation, but I completely lost my shit on him. I told him that I never wanted to see him again, and he started to cry. At that point, he told me that a drunk relative once put a gun to his head and almost killed him, and that this was why he did not trust people easily. I have no idea why he chose that moment to tell me that story. Maybe he thought he could elicit some sympathy from me, but I wasn't feeling very sympathetic, truth be told.

I refused to see him, but I still took his calls. Yes, he had screwed me over fifty ways to Sunday, but his saving grace was that he was always so supportive of my career, almost willing me to believe that there were really no limitations to anything I could accomplish. To this day, it still means a great deal to me.

The last time he called, he left a message on my machine. He said he was in Colorado, and he left a number where he could be reached. I called it, and a woman answered the phone.

"This is Jason returning Tony's call," I said.

"Oh, Jason!" she said. "Tony talks about you all the time! He says you're his best friend!"

"I was never his friend," I said. "I was his lover."

I heard her drop the phone. She picked it back up and started asking me a million questions.

"When?!" "Who?!" "What the…!?"

"You should ask him," I said. And then I hung up and we never spoke again.

Around ten years ago, I got a call from a law enforcement agency asking if I knew Tony's whereabouts. I said I hadn't seen him in twenty years, and then I asked why they were looking for him.

"We can't tell you," they said.

I hung up the phone... asking myself if I ever really knew Tony, or if he ever really loved me. Hours upon hours of therapy, and I still wonder where he is... prison... Colorado... or even a cemetery somewhere. Was he a grifter, or was he a tormented soul who really was in love with me? A part of me still hopes it was the latter.

A couple of years later, still not recovered from how Tony lied to me, I was in Houston, Texas headlining The Laff Stop comedy club. It was the first stop of a Texas Two-Step: I would headline their sister club the very next week in Austin. On the Monday off between club dates, I walked into JR's... a famous gay bar in Houston... and I ordered my usual: Diet Coke (which I don't drink anymore, though I think I still miss it occasionally). This dark and very handsome man, dressed in a Brooks Brothers suit, walked into the bar on this sparsely populated Monday night and started chatting with me. His name was Greg, and he showed genuine interest in me, which produced a mixture of shock and awe.

He looked a little like Burt Reynolds, but he had no mustache so I thought I was in the clear. I went home with him that night and fell fast and furiously in love. He brought me flowers which no one had ever done for me. I now finally understood why Barbra was so crestfallen when Neil Diamond stopped bringing them to her.

Flowers are a big deal!

Greg came to my show every night, and I talked about him on the radio during my morning show appearance that week. It was a huge station and I was a regular, so they got some great ratings while my shows sold out in a heartbeat. It was a fabulous symbiotic relationship.

While on the air, a fan challenged me to kiss Greg on stage, which I did; I'm not one to back down from a challenge. Greg loved it, and the crowd ate it up.

As our relationship progressed, he introduced me to his friends as I started to fly back and forth to see him. We talked all the time by phone, and he even came out to visit me in Los Angeles. I introduced him to my Grandma, Molly, who loved him!

Not since Frank had someone been so kind to me.

When we were out in public, he loved to talk with people and be the center of attention, and that was fine with me because sometimes when you're on stage for a living, you don't necessarily want to be on it for your life. That, and I loved just being his boyfriend... watching him captivate a room the way he captivated me.

Then one day out of nowhere, he stopped returning my calls. I heard from a friend of his that he was in the hospital. I had no idea, but Greg was an alcoholic, and his drinking had gotten him hospitalized. I had very little experience with people who drank that much, so I wasn't sure how to help him, or even what to say to him. My hope was to be with him again when he got better.

Sadly, it was not meant to be. I only saw him once more when I visited Texas again to do a comedy appearance for that very same radio show. He told me that it was over between us, though he never said why.

Greg was the beginning of a series of men who were unavailable, sending me into a downward spiral that culminated in me hitting rock bottom regarding my own self-respect. It was the lowest time of my adult life, and it lasted for over five years. These men ruined me, and me letting them ruin me just made it worse.

I would have to somehow recalibrate myself to learn how to date again and be patient enough to get to know men, while still holding on to what was important for me to respect myself. It's been a fight, it's been my deepest failure, and it's been my greatest triumph to get past it. No longer do I let any man, no matter how attractive, how charming, or how good his kiss is, be in my life unless he treats me with respect and kindness.

It used to be a daily struggle. It no longer is.

# 11

## I'm Comin' Out!

Sometimes when things happen, you don't know what the implications will be to you in terms of your life, and how it will affect who you are and how you operate. I sometimes think of people as a stack of yellow Post-It® Notes, and as events happen in your life, notes of perception stick to you.

You're the guy who got beat up.

You're the guy who got to work with George Clooney.

You're the guy whose parents got divorced.

Yeah, I guess I am that guy.

These notes that stick to us can be dangerous, especially when you start to dwell on them. It's far too easy to become other people's perceptions of yourself. And let's face it, I was a dweller, too often on the pain that I had endured during various moments in my life.

Once there was a note that I simply couldn't shake from my psyche, triggered by being asked to wear a shirt on a television show. When I was in my early thirties, I had my first recurring role in a show called *Sunset Beat* with George Clooney, where he played an undercover cop by day, and the lead singer in a band by night. It was created by Patrick Hasburgh, the same man who created *21 Jump Street*. Patrick really liked me, and he trusted me enough to incorporate some improvisation into my character. It was the first time I ever had the freedom to do that, and it meant a lot.

It was the beginning of me finding my voice as an actor.

Of course, that initial trust may have had something to do with my co-star. I was nervous about getting everything perfect, so I memorized my lines backwards and forwards. As I got to set, I knocked on George's trailer door and asked if we could run our lines together.

He was a lot less famous than he is today, so his presence wasn't so intimidating. He was simply a breathtakingly beautiful, charming, irresistible man.

George said, "You know, let's not worry about the lines. Let's just do what we want."

"Really?" I asked, unsure if he was being serious or just messing with me.

"Trust me."

(Funny side note: I was at a screening of *The Descendants* to see my actor friend Judy Greer who I met and studied with at Jeffrey Tambor's acting class. During the cast Q&A, I raised my hand and said, "George." Judy chimed in before George. "Jason?" As in, "Oh my God, how are you?!" "Whaddya got, Jason?" asked George. "So, George, you're going to get nominated for an Academy Award for this film, but in all the television press briefs, they keep showing you and I together in our scene from *Sunset Beat*. The problem is that in that scene, all you can see is the back of my head. Can you fix that?" "Done," he said without missing a beat. The audience burst into laughter, and it felt like we were back on set together.)

In my scenes with George, I wore this red shirt that looked like a Native American blanket. Apparently, my work on the show was good enough for me to put it on my actor's demo reel. And while it should have brought back a nice memory of my early acting days, it instead elicited a nightmare of the time my uncle Mike attacked me. It was the shirt I was wearing when he ripped it while beating me up.

It was the early 90's, and my grandfather Jack was very ill. He didn't have much time left and everyone knew it. I think he was even looking forward to the end a bit, as he had been missing my grandma Klara who died a few years prior from cancer.

Nerves were frayed and fuses were short as everyone in the family made the sometimes painful pilgrimage that you make as a relative's life is coming to an end... especially so with a patriarch like Jack.

I don't fully remember how the argument started, or even why it started. My uncle Mike and I were going back and forth, and the tension in our discussion was building between us like two trains that were about to crash into each other.

He made a comment. I made a comment.

And then his second wife Micki injected herself into the conversation, saying something to me about being gay, and how my uncle was tired of me bringing it up in every conversation.

I put my hand on her shoulder and said, "This has nothing to do with you."

Without warning, Mike lunged at me and threw me up against the wall, causing me to fall down. Stunned, I picked myself up off the floor and ran into the other room, with him following suit. The only power I felt I had at the time was my words, so I yelled a few things at him that I can't quite remember but would probably regret if I did. Mike was so angry that he started to choke me.

You know it's bad when the man you're visiting on his deathbed has to be the one to break it up. Jack came into the room and gave us a look as if to say, "Really? Here? Now?"

I found my way out of the apartment, angry and scared and raging, which is probably why I did not see Mike's son, my cousin Mitch, following me. As I walked into the courtyard outside the building, he pushed me down and kicked me.

Mitch was considered "the good grandson" in the family. My grandma Klara always used to say to me, "Why can't you be more like Mitchell?"

"Because I'm not him," I would retort. "I'm me."

And at that moment, I was on the ground while he was standing over me like a bully.

I couldn't fathom the events that had just unfolded, and I was officially persona non grata after that day. I know that Jack was the focus of why people were there in the first place, but I was hoping that someone would call to see if I was okay.

No one did, not even my own dad, who wasn't even there when this… what I would call gay-bashing… occurred.

Shortly after everything went down, Mitch reached out to me to profusely apologize. He said his reason was that he was so upset about our grandfather being ill and that his emotions got the better of him. I forgave him and we made peace with each other. And to this day, our relationship has flourished.

It would take my uncle Mike a lot longer to reconnect with me. He had the same outlook that my father had: "Why can't you be gay and shut up about it?"

What he didn't understand was that I was just trying to figure out who I was, and coming to any kind of concrete terms was extremely confusing. I grew up in a closet, under a doormat. I was like a weed trying to look for any shred of light just to survive.

Think about the concept of living in the closet. You're in a small room, standing on the shoes, behind the leather jacket… with hat boxes and shit above you. Every once in a while, someone opens up the door, flashes a light in your eyes, takes something out, and then slams it shut. And this is how you make all your decisions, and I was so tired of making decisions that way. I couldn't do it anymore.

In 1990, I had just come off a role in *Kindergarten Cop* opposite Arnold Schwarzenegger who was a massive box office star at that time. I had cultivated a very successful feature-act gig in comedy clubs all over the country. I had even just done a successful spot on Showtime's Comedy Club Network that was generating a lot of buzz.

On the surface, I was on top of the world. But as anyone in the closet will tell you, we live beneath the surface. Even with the success I was building, I was so unhappy. I knew that the act I was doing had no future. Even my look was hopeless. I would spike up my hair and wear leopard jackets and zebra pants. I even donned a purple lame jacket on *Star Search* while dancing around a circle on the stage… just because I didn't want anybody to know I was gay.

There I was… hiding in plain sight.

I felt I had nowhere to go as an artist, with no place to talk about myself as an adult. Everything seemed to be about the past. I would joke about my punk rock girlfriend. "Yeah, I give her my hand to help her out of the car. She put her cigarette out in it. Girls don't find me sexually stimulating. I don't know why."

But the crowd loved it more than the comedian.

I thought that I had to stay where I was. As an actor in the early 90's, coming out was considered career suicide. One slip-up, and all my hopes and dreams of being a character actor would instantly evaporate. I was told this by just about everyone.

In a funny twist of fate, I got an offer to do stand-up comedy on a gay cruise, and I figured that since it was in the middle of the ocean, who would know? It would be an easy place to hide and maybe try out a new joke or two about being gay. So I did the job and I got to meet the incomparable Harvey Fierstein, and while it was not my worst work ever, I had very little material on being openly gay… which is apparently important to have when you're playing to an exclusively gay audience.

But being so naïve and so out of my comfort zone, I was fired after doing only two of the four booked cruises. I learned that if you're going to be openly gay, you actually have to talk about it. Who knew?

Oy!

So for the next year, I buckled down and I worked on some new material about my actual self. It was cathartic and nerve-racking and exhilarating and terrifying. It was nothing I wanted, and everything I needed.

So as luck would have it, I got a call from Budd Friedman who owned the famous Improv comedy clubs. He asked me if I would do an AIDS benefit at their Chicago club. I could not say no, especially to a legend like Budd. And I so wanted to be supportive of the AIDS community.

When I told a friend about Budd's call, he asked me if Budd thought I was gay.

Everyone knew… even before I did.

But I couldn't admit it to myself; there were so many things to consider besides my career. Once, I went to Los Angeles Gay Pride with a man I was dating at the time. I remember seeing the parents of gays and lesbians, and I choked back tears. The idea that a parent would walk with their son or daughter in this celebration of pride in public moved me to the core of who I was as a person.

Long after that man and I had broken up, I still continued to go to Gay Pride. One time, I was walking back to the parking structure of the Beverly Center where I had parked my car. I saw Ellen DeGeneres and a very sporty looking gal coming up the escalator of the garage. I knew Ellen a little bit; I had opened for her previously at The Improv in San Diego, the year she appeared on *The Tonight Show Starring Johnny Carson* for the very first time in the mid-eighties.

I remember on the day of her appearance, as she was a hundred miles away in Burbank taping the show, I snuck into her bedroom of the comedy condo where we were staying to see if both beds in her room were being used by her and a girl… friend… who accompanied her for the week-long engagement. All the luggage was on one bed; the other bed was unmade.

I knew it!

And I was relieved by it. I was not alone; we were both closeted comedians.

So now on that day on the escalator, as I saw Ellen coming with another similar gal to the one in San Diego, both of them wearing tank tops and shorts on that summer day, I innocently asked, "Were you both at Pride?"

"Oh gosh, I could never do that," Ellen replied. "What if someone should see me?"

"Oh, yeah… well… nice to see you again," was all I could muster.

I was speechless, which was so unlike me. Here she was… afraid that someone would see her wearing a tank top and shorts like everyone else on a warm summer's day. She thought if it made the news, her and a gal-pal walking together looking the way they did, that it would end her career. I thought long and hard about what I saw, and I thought about those moms and dads walking proudly with their children, and I said to myself, 'This is not the life that I want. This is not who I wanna be.'

So I went to Chicago and I did my show where I talked about being gay, and it was one of the most exhilarating experiences I'd ever had. I was so empowered that the very next day, with the help of my dear friend, actress and comedian Marcie Smolin, I sent out a press release through my fax machine to all the popular talk shows: Geraldo Rivera, Sally Jesse Raphael, Phil Donahue, Oprah Winfrey, Jenny Jones, you name it… offering my closet-virginity, if you will. I needed Marcie's help to make it sound coherent (she's a really good writer as well as an acting coach), as I was already behind the eight ball being a product of the Los Angeles public school system.

Geraldo and Sally Jesse responded that they were interested. At that time, Geraldo was even more popular than Oprah was. It's amazing what a chair to the face will do for your career (see: the KKK episode). And since this was going to be a fairly exclusive announcement, I had to go with the biggest audience. Geraldo would be my date.

The producers wanted to create a show around me coming out. The show was titled Unconventional Comedians, and along with me would feature Paul Mooney as the Angry Black Comedian, Kathy Buckley as the Hearing Impaired Comedian, Sandy Church as the Little Person Comedian, and my best friend, Sheila Kay, as the I Lost a Shit-Ton of Weight Comedian. Apart from Paul, I suggested all the other comedians for the episode, and if I'm being honest, Sheila really didn't lose that much weight… I just really wanted her on the show!

The episode was a gimmick. What you need to realize is that all comedians are unconventional. These were just easy artifices for the audience to grasp, all wrapped up in a nice little bow. And it provided me a vehicle for what I needed to do.

So in June of 1993, I walked out of the closet and I stepped into the light… leading me to be the man I am today. I remember everything and nothing of what happened that day. Some moments are blurry, but some are crystal clear. And looking at the episode with my eyes much clearer today, I see just how ready I was.

I was new to being so public about my sexual orientation, but even when faced with a question from the audience by an older woman who seemed to be afraid that I would soon be having sex in public in front of her grandchildren, I didn't bat an eye. I slowly and methodically explained to her that just because you're gay doesn't mean that you lose your morals.

She said that she didn't want children to see two men kissing, that kids would be curious about it. I asked her what she thought was going to happen if they did, and she couldn't answer the question.

And then I asked her if she was comfortable kissing her husband in public. At first, the question seemed to flummox her, but as it finally dawned on her what I was asking, she said, "Yes, I would kiss him in front of other people."

"Then why can't I have the same right?" I asked.

Sixteen minutes out of the closet and already I was an advocate. I can't say I saw that coming. And I really didn't expect the success that followed after the show aired. It was the beginning of creating a series of tours that led to most of my success in the 90's and the early 2000's.

After I was long out, and ten years after that fateful afternoon at my grandfather Jack's deathbed, my uncle Mike showed up at my apartment, unannounced, his hat in hand. And that day, at that moment, as he apologized to me, all I could do was forgive him. There was nothing else to do.

It was never the same though. I think I wanted to hold onto my animosity for Mike, but I just couldn't. He was such a mixed bag. When I first moved out on my own, I would get a twenty-dollar cashier's check every month for the first two years I lived alone in my first bachelor apartment. It was the epitome of opulence, with a Murphy bed, a kitchen with no sink, and a shower where I washed my body… and my dishes… at the same time.

For years, I worried that I'd have to send the money back. There was no name on it. I only found out later that it was Mike who was looking out for me. He wanted to see me land on my feet, but he knew I wouldn't take money, and that I wanted to do it on my own. It was the better part of five hundred dollars over two years, and it really helped me out a lot. I will always be grateful for that simple act of generosity.

My uncle died recently. He was a heavy smoker, so how he lasted as long as he did I'll never know. And in some of his dying words he said to me, "I just want you to know that I'm not gay, and I was never attracted to you."

Seriously.

As I sat in the room with his two children, Mitch and Anne, we all stared at each other in disbelief and laughed. Sometimes, things just don't make any sense. Sometimes, they don't need to.

# 12

# They Say That Blood Is Thicker Than Water... Not

My sister Karen was born almost four years after me. She was the first and only one of us to be born in Los Angeles. She was the little girl that both of my parents had always wanted, but especially in my father's eyes, she could do no wrong.

Growing up, until our teen years, she always seemed to look up to me and wanted to spend time with me. As she became a tween herself, reverence turned to embarrassment as she was forced to answer questions about my sexual preference. She insisted that I wasn't gay to her friends.

Karen always seemed to be searching for her place... where she would fit in, who she would be. When she was very young, my dad took an old eight-millimeter film of her wearing her sweater backwards and riding an old tricycle when there was a new one given to her for her birthday. I think this, somewhat, summed up her personality perfectly.

She started to chase boys at a younger age than most at that time, when she was thirteen or fourteen. She would meet a boy, fall in love with a boy, and become who that boy wanted her to be. She was like a mood ring.

This pattern coincided right around the time when my parents got divorced. I was seventeen when it happened. Even though my mother had been having an on-and-off affair with George the butcher for fifteen years of her twenty-two-year marriage, it was unbeknownst to me. I was thrilled that the George and Martha *Who's Afraid of Virginia Woolf?* marriage was finally coming to an end. All that drama was not going to be a part of our lives anymore, and we could all just breathe.

When my father was packing his stuff to move out, he walked into the kitchen to ask my mother which dishes he could take to his new apartment.

"Take whatever you want," she said and walked out.

Five minutes later, she walked back in and she saw that he was taking the white dishes with the blue rose and silver trim that she used when company came over. She had saved for almost a year to purchase them with Blue Chip stamps. In her best Joan Crawford voice, she wailed, "You're taking everything!"

She pulled down the rack from the cabinet and threw the dishes at him like a Greek at a dinner party after way too much Ouzo. It was the final exclamation point of the story of their marriage... which if it was to be turned into a film would be called Lying, Cheating and Stealing.

This divorce affected my sister much more than it affected me. Even though I was happy this film had finally left the theatre, she was only thirteen at the time while I was seventeen. Being older, I always understood that this was never going to work, but I think she felt that our family could somehow stay together.

She and I ended up living with my mom, but I left them less than a year later, two months after my eighteenth birthday.

As the years went on, in between boyfriends, she would call me and we would hang out, go to movies, eat deli food, and she would even come to watch my shows at the comedy clubs with her friends. These times were very close to my heart. But invariably, she would find another boy, and I would find myself back out in the cold.

After a few different boyfriends, she rented a house with several roommates that was owned by a religious Jewish man who introduced her to a man from Israel, named Ronnie. From the moment I met Ronnie, I felt an uneasy sense of negativity emanating from him to me.

My sister had had boyfriends of all different types, so I thought Ronnie would be just another phase she was going through. Again, I could not have been more wrong. When they first met, he was religious but not overly devout. They even lived together before they were married. But by the time the wedding occurred, they were full-blown Orthodox Jews. I was told to come to the wedding, not bring up the past, wear something conservative… and a hat.

So I wore all black, a bolo tie, and a cowboy hat. I'm such a smartass. What was I thinking?

At the wedding, my sister treated me like I was a stranger, as was my mother and grandmother, Molly. I wasn't introduced to any of his family, and people constantly asked me who I was. I had to explain to them that I was the brother of the bride, and I wasn't a cowboy. Kidding!

The next few years were tense, and I was not welcomed into their lives. I remember a distinct time at my cousin Mitch's daughter's birthday party at Chuck E. Cheese when Ronnie asked me, "Why don't you find a nice girl and settle down?"

It was so insulting, and a catalyst for my withdrawal from their lives more and more.

The real break came when my sister was pregnant with their first child. She became cold and distant, and didn't seem to want me around. I was nothing but a fading memory during her second pregnancy when she gave birth to twins. Soon after, my father told me that she moved to Israel, where she would eventually have another daughter… their fourth child. Oy!

After a few years of living there, they realized that making money was tight. So they moved back to the States, where my father helped them buy a house. She called me one day while I was on the exercise bike, saying, "I'm living back in Los Angeles now. We can see each other, but you won't be able to come to our house, and you won't be allowed to see the children. I could meet you in a park."

I stopped pedaling and got off the bike, stunned. She made me feel like I was a Russian spy. And the reason, of course, was because I was gay, and she didn't want me to influence her kids into my gay lifestyle.

Lifestyle?

It felt like she thought I had a disco ball in my living room, and that men would be coming and going as if it was an amusement park. She was also frightened of me telling her children anything about her past indiscretions. It's like she didn't want them to think she was human or had a past or a brother, me. I was pretty upset, we fought, and we hung up on each other.

This complete breakdown of communication between my sister and I caused quite a stir for my family, especially my dad. How would be spend the holidays? Who would be invited to what? I was often not included in family events, only to find out later that my sister was.

We didn't speak until 2004, when my grandmother Molly died. I had been taking care of her for the final years of her life. I would take her to doctors' appointments, I was a mainstay at her retirement hotel, and I even handled the final arrangements for her funeral. Since my mom had moved to Palm Springs, I was now her person... you know, like they are in *Grey's Anatomy*.

On the day of Molly's funeral, my sister showed up and the first thing she said was that the poster board of pictures and memories of my grandmother that I had created with my mom was very goysha... which is a swipe at me being the "bad Jew," while she was one of the "chosen people" because she had become an Orthodox Jew.

When we were in the chapel, almost all my friends came and told stories of my grandmother. During those last years, she would come with me to parties at friends' houses to celebrate holidays, and they adored her... as they do my mother now. She actually knew my friend Lydia and her daughter Lexie better than she knew her own great-grandchildren.

The last two years of my grandmother's life, I moved her to a nursing home in Palm Springs so that she could be closer to my mom. Both of them said that they didn't think they could handle that much contact after so many years apart, but it became a love fest.

However, my grandmother had one stipulation before she would move into the nursing home: she didn't want to share a room with anyone who was black. Though she loved all my African American friends, including Lexie whom she treated as if she was her own great-grandchild, she drew her line in the sand.

Her first roommate was a woman who could not stop complaining, and Molly could not stand her. Her second roommate was a woman who barely spoke. The quiet drove Molly crazy. And then there was Eunice from Atlanta. They became best friends and were like two peas in a pod.

And guess what? She was black. They became so close that when Eunice moved back to Atlanta, they kept in touch through cards and letters. I guess you can teach an old dog new tricks.

My grandmother's favorite song was *Over the Rainbow*, and she asked me to play it at her funeral. For some odd reason, the CD player would not work. Even though I'm not a singer, I would often sing to her, so my mom asked me to sing it acapella. Oy!

Nonetheless, it was very heartfelt, there were tears, and it was a wonderful tribute to Molly.

When we moved to the gravesite, my sister decided to sit next to me… pushing her way into our family as if she'd been a part of my grandmother's life.

FYI… my sister had rarely gone to see Molly, and she brought her children to visit at the retirement hotel even less. Molly barely got to know them or visit with them. She wasn't asked to come to my sister's house for the holidays, and for all intents and purposes, she was treated like a complete stranger. I guess my grandmother had a part in it, too. It upset her deeply the way my sister treated my mother and me, and she was not quiet about it.

So at the gravesite, as they lowered my grandmother into the ground, my sister sitting to my left, my mom to my right, my blood was boiling. I held it in though, and sat there until everyone had left. As I walked my mom back to the car, my sister made the mistake of walking past me. I looked at her and yelled in my best Joan Collins from *Dynasty* delivery, "You broke your grandmother's hearrrrrrrt!"

We went at it back and forth, and I told her to get away from me and that she wasn't welcome here.

"I am!" she yelled. "I'm part of this family, too!"

"You're a thoughtless bitch!" I screamed.

She then smacked me across my face. I then pulled her wig off. As my good friend Lydia drove away with her daughter Lexie, she stopped the car and yelled at me, "Get back in your car. Get back in your car and go home! Just... go... home!" She was trying to help me, but it was too late at that point. I was out of my mind with grief and resentment.

As bad as that day was, the next day was worse. My brother and his wife and daughter had driven in from Las Vegas to attend the funeral. I put them up in the guest room of my apartment so that they wouldn't have to pay for a hotel room. My mom was sleeping in my bedroom, and I was sleeping on the couch in the living room. It was a full house, but believe me, not like the TV show.

After the fight between my sister and myself at the funeral, the whole family was in full combat gear, taking sides on who was right, who was wrong, and who was just five minutes from an OJ trial. The day after the funeral was Thanksgiving, which the Orthodox Jews didn't celebrate, and somehow, my sister convinced everyone (but me) to come to her house to see the grandchildren.

I had ordered a Thanksgiving dinner to be picked up and served at five o'clock. My brother said that he and his family, along with our mom, would only be spending a couple of hours with my sister… just to see the grandchildren… and they would be back in time for dinner. It was noon when they left.

So it's the day after my grandmother… who was like my second mother… was buried, and there I was in my apartment, all alone. By coincidence, *Funny Girl* was playing on TV. I watched it and cried for three hours straight.

Barbra to my rescue once again!

I left to pick up the dinner, expecting them to be back when I returned. I came home with armloads of food to an empty apartment. Around six o'clock, I was beside myself. And of course, I couldn't call to see where they were because I was still at DEFCON One with my sister.

I felt betrayed by my family… once again an outsider. As they walked into my apartment later that night, I was so upset. I likened myself to a dog who'd been put outside for barking too much. When I told my mother my feelings, she apologized profusely and said that she didn't want to lose her relationship with her grandchildren… which she later did, anyway. My brother, as usual, thought that I was overreacting and too emotional. This scenario would go on for years… me setting myself up for letdown after letdown by both my brother and my sister.

My brother had been mad at me since… let's say… the day I was born. He stopped speaking to me civilly the night that Barbra Streisand lost the Oscar for *The Way We Were* to Glenda Jackson in *A Touch of Class* in 1974.

I'm kidding, but that's how it felt. I could do no right with either of them for most of my life.

When I was a kid, all I wanted to do was hang out with my brother and for him to like me. I'm not sure he ever did. We shared a room in the early years of our childhood on Maryland Drive, but the house was eventually torn down, much like our family. One year, my brother wanted a Polaroid camera for his birthday, and my mom said that she would get him one if he would give me his old camera. It was one of those instamatic cameras that you could put a flashbulb in at the top for indoor shots.

I did not know that he and my mom worked out that arrangement, so without her knowing, he told me that if I would be his slave for one whole day, that he would give me his old camera. I jumped at the chance. He made me walk behind him at all times that day, among other indignities. When my mother found out about these and many more events, she had a conniption.

He was allowed to keep the Polaroid, however, and I got his old camera.

He also once made me put my hand in a bucket of quick-dry cement, which completely hardened in a matter of minutes. I thought it was hilarious at the time. When my mother drove up in her 1968 mint-green Camaro from shopping (or one of her affairs; it's hard to remember), he tried to chop it off with an axe and almost cut my hand off.

At that point, it didn't seem so hilarious anymore. I was scared shitless. The axe worked, but he ended up nicking me, causing a scar that lasted well into my twenties, though you can't even see it anymore.

For years, he wouldn't let me go to sleep until I could guess what he was thinking. I actually thought this was something that was possible to do. I was three years younger than him, meaning I was three years more gullible. Yet for all the times I gave in to my brother's torture, I still couldn't make him like me.

Over the years, he would stop talking to me and almost everyone in our family. You needed a map, a GPS, and a PowerPoint to figure out who the hell he was talking to or not talking to at any given time. I spent most of my thirties and forties apologizing to both my brother and sister to try and clear up the wreckage of my past, and to figure out what was my part in these damaged relationships.

With my sister, it seems irrevocable. No matter what I do or say, nothing seems to change. I still can't understand completely her private rendition of *Fiddler on the Roof* that she's been living in for the last thirty years. I really don't know who she is anymore.

My brother is a different story. I've come to be at peace, knowing that his road has not been easy. He and his wife have one child, and she was born with severe mental issues. It has made it hard for him to have relationships outside of his wife and daughter.

I've learned to accept who they are, and their limitations. I've moved on… and I'm honestly okay about it.

# 13

## The Mentor and the Mentee

I grew up in a movie theatre. I spent hours and hours and hours going to the movies, watching them, imbibing them, making them a part of my own DNA, and in my own mind, being in them. One of my earliest memories is going to see *The Sound of Music* at the Carthay Circle Theatre, one of those long-lost gorgeous Hollywood movie palaces. It was a glorious building to say the least. Sadly, it was torn down to make way for God-knows-what, but in its demise, the public outcry paved the way for the preservation of other historic buildings in Los Angeles.

In front of the theatre was a large grassy area where, after seeing Julie Andrews in all her glory, I chose to re-create the moment by belting out, "The hills are alive!" for all to hear. This was the start of my acting career. I bought the soundtrack on record, which I still have, and I memorized all the words to *Edelweiss* that Christopher Plummer made famous.

Growing up feeling so alone in so many ways, I used to think I didn't have a lot of mentors; the truth is that I really did, only they didn't know they were my mentors at the time. There they were... up on the big screen and on the small one in my bedroom. There were just so many performances that I saw which changed me. The first one, other than Barbra in *Funny Girl* of course, was probably Dustin Hoffman in *Midnight Cowboy*. I could not believe the same man who played the freshly scrubbed college man in *The Graduate* was the same one who played Ratso Rizzo. I was so moved by the friendship that Ratso had with Jon Voight's Joe Buck. They were so close, it was like they were a couple.

Dare to dream!

And that film was so groundbreaking. Tame by today's standards, *Midnight Cowboy* was originally rated X, and it still won the Academy Award for best picture in 1970. Of course, I didn't get to see the film in its unedited glory. I had to settle for television because I wasn't old enough to go to the theatre.

One performance that pushed me over the edge was Gena Rowlands in *A Woman Under the Influence*, which was directed by her husband John Cassavetes. They were both nominated for Oscars. My acting coach at the time, Lawrence Parke, said, "If you don't go see Gena Rowlands in the movie, you can't come back to this class."

The film was about a blue-collar woman trapped in a marriage in the 1970's, stuck in a life to which she had no control, nor any idea how she really got there in the first place. I took my mom to see it when I saw it for the second time, and she said, "I don't need to go to the movies to see my life." I think she liked it though, and how could she not? Gena inhabited that role like no other actor I'd ever seen. It was almost like watching a documentary!

I recently talked about this film with a young actress I had been mentoring, and she could not understand why Gena Rowlands' character went crazy, just because she had to stay home to be a wife and mother. In 1974 when this movie came out, women had much fewer choices. Either you worked, or you were a mother… but you couldn't do both. And if you weren't planning on having children, at least at first, a woman may have felt that not only was her life over as she knew it, but that… in a sense… who she was didn't exist anymore. When my own mother signed her checks, she wrote Mrs. Leonard Greif on the line for her name. She couldn't even sign her own name, in part because it just wasn't done at that time.

Another film that killed me was *They Shoot Horses, Don't They?* starring Jane Fonda. It was the other film playing in a double feature with the one that I begged my parents to take me to with Marlo Thomas called *Jenny*. She was one of the biggest stars at the time from the TV show *That Girl*, where she played a New York actress who had a fabulous apartment and seemingly no job to pay for it. *Jenny* also featured a little known actor at the time named Alan Alda. The movie itself was okay; it was about an unwed mother-to-be who marries a total stranger who is trying to avoid the draft. These were the issues of the day.

After *Jenny*, I ran to get more popcorn for the second feature, which had already been out earlier that year. At ten years old, I was so young that I didn't know that it had been nominated for nine Oscars; I just thought it was a film with Jane Fonda... an actress I barely knew.

The movie took place in the 1930's dance halls. Long since banned, there used to be these contests where the organizers would make people dance until they dropped, and whomever could dance the longest would either win a contract with a movie studio or a bag of money. It was a huge deal during the Great Depression.

It was also the first time that I was to understand the depth of my sadness as a child. Here laid bare before me on the silver screen was a story about people desperate to be in show business, trapped in a life from where there was no escape. At the end of the film, Jane asks her dance partner to shoot her. When her dance partner asks why, she says, "They shoot horses, don't they?"

It's what they do to horses when they are in so much pain, when they are so broken and nothing can fix them. And often, as a child, I felt that way emotionally. But seeing people act out feelings that only I thought existed gave me hope... gave me something to search for. Just the fact that I could let my feelings out in a darkened movie theatre gave me the strength to keep moving forward toward my goal of being an actor.

These movies kept me alive.

But sadness and pain wasn't all I was drawn to in films. I remember seeing Barbra and Ryan O'Neal in *What's Up, Doc?* and laughing my head off. It also introduced me to some of the best character actors in the business, people I'd seen on TV shows, and some who were about to hit the big time. Madeline Kahn, Kenneth Mars, Austin Pendleton, Mabel Anderson, John Hillerman, and a very young Randy Quaid. It was Madeline Kahn's first film. John Hillerman went on to fame in *Magnum, P.I.* Mabel Anderson was Darren's mom on *Bewitched.* Austin Pendleton became an incredible character actor and director on Broadway. Randy Quaid would go on to be nominated for an academy award for *The Last Detail* the very next year. I began to see the artistry of these amazing character portrayals, and it opened up a new reality... a virtual doorway... for what I thought I wanted to do with my life.

In a way, certain people in certain films made me feel like there was space for me. I often felt like I was a plant growing under a doormat. Occasionally, someone would pick up the mat that would give me some sun. Without that sunlight, I would have just continued to grow like a weed in all different directions, never knowing which road to take to lead me to something more.

Films like *Julia* with Jane Fonda and Vanessa Redgrave; it was the first time I saw a story about someone standing up and risking everything for a friend by smuggling funds through Nazi Germany to support others in need.

And then there was *Ordinary People,* with incomparable performances from Mary Tyler Moore and Donald Sutherland. Only she could play that part... America's sweetheart as the worst mother alive. It was the first time that I saw crystal clearly how you could transform yourself into a completely different character from the one you thought was reality. The hard lines were now blurred, and in some ways, erased. It was a thrilling revelation.

It was also a film that terrified me in a way, as I related dangerously close to Timothy Hutton's character. It was about someone my age who survives unbearable grief, and who is able to let go of the wreckage of his past and be honest with himself that he's powerless over who is mother is. Not that my mother was anything like Mary Tyler Moore's character… thank God!

I've seen the film well over ten times, which is most likely my record.

One night after a workshop with a bunch of my closeted gay actor friends, we discussed *Ordinary People* and talked about our hopes and dreams. We were all going to make it big… or so we thought. As of today, one has left the business entirely. One works as an extra with small roles, one produces and still acts a bit.

And then there's me.

They're now all out of the closet and more comfortable in their own skin, though I think for most of us, it's still a battle to succeed. For one of the others, it was easier just to walk away.

But for me, walking away was not an option. There was too much inspiration and too much beauty to simply pack it in. I clung to the artists who changed me. Dustin Hoffman may always be my favorite, from *Lenny* to *Kramer vs. Kramer* to *Tootsie* to *Rain Man* to *American Buffalo* to *Wag the Dog* to *Last Chance Harvey* to *The Meyerowitz Stories*… and even to *Meet the Fockers* with you know who. There's always so much joy in his performances.

But sometimes, it's not just a character who moves me. Every now and then, a movie will change me because of the deeper meaning of what it's about. *Field of Dreams* did that for me. It made me realize that if you build it…

… it will come. It was a reminder that there was a way through it if you hold on tight and don't let go… just like at the end of *Ordinary People*.

Do you remember the scene in *Field of Dreams* where Kevin Costner's dad asks him, "Do you want to have a catch?" Most people use that metaphor as an affirmation for the love of baseball between a father and a son. For me, it was a moment that unlocked a sense of forgiveness that I needed to give my dad for not being emotionally available to me while I was growing up… which is what I really wanted from him. In no uncertain terms, *Field of Dreams* gave me permission to forgive my father.

When I was in junior high, my dad would have to pass my school to go to work every morning. He would always stop by the farmers' market to get a cup of coffee and a donut, which would always make us late, which would then induce a bad grade for me in citizenship, which would always make my mom angry with me. I could have taken the bus every morning and be on time, but I would have rather been late… so long as I could be with my dad. It took, "Do you want to have a catch?" to begin my healing years later.

And that's what movies, TV, and the theater gave me: the education that school could not. I couldn't focus on studying from the constant mistreatment directed at me on a daily basis. For me, school wasn't about learning; it was about surviving. Sometimes, just seeing someone who was different owning who they are, either as a character or their real-life persona, was enough to make a day not seem so shitty.

Whoopi Goldberg did that for me in *The Color Purple*. She was such an original, so unlike anyone who wasn't her, and I knew that if she could work, so could I. She stood up loudly and said, "This is who I am." My favorite performances of hers were *The Long Walk Home*… a movie about the civil rights movement which also starred Sissy Spacek, and *Corrina, Corrina*… a film about the relationship of Jews and African Americans in the 1950's. I felt this incredible connection between us that lives inside me to this day.

When I finally got a place at the table, I made the decision to observe, ingest, and when appropriate, seek out anything and everything from so many wonderful people who have been, and would be, such a huge influence on me. Like Lin-Manuel Miranda so beautifully said, "I'm not going to throw away my shot!"

And because of that openness and hard work, I've had the good fortune of working with and learning from some incredible stars. I got to act with the Oscar-nominated actress Carroll Baker, who played the deliciously villainous domineering mother of Richard Tyson in *Kindergarten Cop*. I had to take rollers out of her hair during the filming, but she didn't want me to touch her hair.

What was I to do? Oy!

Before filming one day, she mentioned that she'd lost her reading glasses. As it happened, we were filming in a mall at a big hair salon in Santa Ana, California. I found an eyewear place in the mall where she could buy a new pair. We became fast friends, and for the rest of the shoot, I hung out in her trailer. We stayed in contact for years, and she was the first actor who ever let me improv with her in a scene.

I worked with the brilliant Laurie Metcalf on the sitcom *Norm*. I had one scene which morphed into two. Laurie was in the second scene. Watching her work was an acting lesson… her commitment, her use of action, taking an idea and going for it… made a huge impression on me.

I also did a film called *Ghosts Never Sleep* with the notorious Faye Dunaway. I played a talk show host who ambushes her character. It was one long scene with another short scene afterwards, both with her. The first time I saw her on the set, she was walking with a cane and wearing a dowdy woman's suit with her hair pulled back into a bun. Her character spoke with a slight Irish brogue, as did Faye at that moment; she was totally in character.

I asked if there was anything I could do specifically for her in the scene, but she was all business and said, "Let's just run it," in her slight Irish brogue.

I was ready for her. After we "just ran it," she completely changed and became totally available to me. It really taught me that if you are prepared in your work, other people notice. When it came time to do my coverage (which means my close-ups, after we'd already done hers), she stayed to act with me, even though she was not on camera. Many famous actors leave for coverage… she didn't, and she could not have been more complimentary.

It means a lot to actors when this happens. The late Michael Clarke Duncan once credited earning an Academy Award nomination to Tom Hanks for staying for coverage for him during filming of *The Green Mile*. Haley Joel Osment said the same thing about Bruce Willis after his Academy Award nomination for *The Sixth Sense*.

In the late 1990's, I got to do a movie for HBO called *Gia*, starring a then-little-known actress named Angelina Jolie. The film was written and directed by Michael Cristofer, who won the Pulitzer Prize for writing the play *The Shadow Box*. In real life, Gia was a famous model and one of the first lesbians who died of AIDS. In the film, I got to do three short scenes where I played Gia's agent. I remember having a conversation with Angie, as she was called, and her telling me that she was unsure of her taking this role because it was so emotionally draining and difficult. She was afraid she wouldn't do it justice.

I told her she was crazy, that this was a great opportunity and she should just go for it. Geez, where did I get the chutzpa?

This was the film that changed her career; she was nominated for an Emmy, and she won a Golden Globe for her portrayal. When we had the cast and crew screening, she walked across the room to actually say hello to me. The only other big star who did that for me was Rosie O'Donnell after I saw her in an Off-Broadway play called *Love, Loss, and What I Wore* written by Nora and Delia Ephron. Though Rosie was a peer and later hired me to perform stand-up on her R Family Vacations cruise, it meant a lot to me; she and Angie were both so supportive and truly class acts.

I was lucky enough to get to work in a couple of plays with great ensembles. One was *P.A.N.I.C. in Griffith Park*. It was written by David Reid, and was directed by my pal, actress Lee Garlington. It was about the politico, Lyndon LaRouche, who put forth an initiative to lock up people who had AIDS or were HIV positive. This play was born to combat that. It was also a life-changing experience, as I'd never played a gay person before.

There were times when I was so scared that I couldn't breathe. I was frightened that my whole career would be over if people found out I was gay. Some of the people in the play, at that time, were closeted. I'd never been involved in something so politically charged. Little did I know that it was the beginning of my activism.

I remember the producer Ian Praiser, who has since left the planet, would sit with me and virtually hold my hand and tell me how powerful my work was, and how this would change me as an actor. He was one of the writer-producers on the TV show *Taxi*, one of the most transformative shows in television history, so his words came with a great deal of pedigree. I'd never had anyone of that stature speak to me in that way, and it meant the world.

Woody Harrelson also came to see the show, and I believe he put a little money into it. He also had some very kind words for me and my performance. He told me that being who I was in the play is where it has the most meaning, and it gave me permission to create a sense of vulnerability in my performance.

When I saw the film *The Trip to Bountiful* starring actress Geraldine Page, it was a revelation to me. It showed me how the depth of a performance could change someone in literally every way... not just the inside like Mary Tyler Moore, but also the outside... the actual physical body, the accent, the emotion, everything. It's hard to believe that this old woman who just wanted to go back to her home in Bountiful, was also a New York intellectual socialite in Woody Allen's *Interiors*, who did everything she could to keep from having a nervous breakdown because a lamp was not in the right place.

Over thirty years later, I can still say that there are just so many people who mentored me in ways big and small, without them even knowing it, and who continue to do so today. The power of Denzel Washington in *The Hurricane*. The depth of Alfre Woodard and Mary McDonnell in *Passion Fish*. The comic artistry of Lily Tomlin in *The Late Show*. The humanity of Karl Malden... and actually everyone... in *A Streetcar Named*

*Desire.* The transformation and dedication to the character of Hilary Swank in *Boys Don't Cry.* The unabashed commitment of a character's appearance with Cloris Leachman in *Young Frankenstein.* The passion and sensitivity of helping to give a voice to the voiceless of Nate Parker in *The Birth of a Nation.*

And Meryl Streep in literally anything.

These are but a few of the people who have mentored me, and there are so many more I can't even begin to list. All of them have held me in their virtual arms as an artist. And because of them, I was able to not feel so alone as a child, and to see the possibilities for a place to be safe in the world of being an actor, and even as a human being.

So I say to you, watch these performances and more. They will change you. They changed me, and led me to giving back... to be present for those who take the time to ask me for help or guidance. I once had an assistant ask me, "Why do you take everybody's call and answer every piece of e-mail yourself?"

"Because it takes just a few minutes every day to give back a little," I said.

And this is why I mentor people of all ages. I think it's our duty as elders to give our experience, strength, and hope to fellow men and women who need them. It's deeply fun and rewarding to share in someone's success. Even just a call to a fellow artist to say congrats for their accomplishments makes a difference. It always does for me when I receive that call, text, or e-mail.

It's an easy thing to take someone by the hand... to encourage them... to believe in them even when they don't believe in themselves. In the film *Orphans,* which was so brilliantly written by Lyle Kessler, the late Sir Albert Finney said how giving someone a gentle squeeze helps them know that you're there for them.

# 14

## Keep Your Friends Close and
## Your Enemies in A Storage Locker

So in the late 1980's, I had a fan-boy crush on a comedian and actor named Taylor Negron. You might remember him as "Milo," the psychopathic bad guy in the Bruce Willis and Damon Wayans film *The Last Boy Scout*. He was also the pizza delivery man who brought a double cheese and sausage to Sean Penn's Spicoli in *Fast Times at Ridgemont High*. People were always saying that I was like a younger version of him (even though he was only two years older than me); I think it was because he started in stand-up comedy so much earlier. He was smart, eccentric, funny, and definitely an original. Because I was compared to him so often, I purposely didn't watch his stand-up a lot because I didn't want to get any of his material to pop into my head.

Of course, growing up at a similar time meant that every once in a while we had similar thoughts. We both told a joke about *Bewitched*, and the fact that they switched Dicks on us. From actor Dick York to Dick Sargent. As if we wouldn't notice. For years, he was mad at me about it; I had no idea that it was part of his act, nor did I even realize that he knew I was alive... much less mad about my Dick joke.

We would run into each other at parties and auditions, and I think the fact that I was openly gay publicly made him uncomfortable because he never officially came out. He came out much the same way Lily Tomlin did: by sauntering.

We sometimes auditioned against each other for the same roles. At one point, he even replaced me on a film, *The Fluffer*, and I replaced him on another, *Puff, Puff, Pass*. Neither of us appreciated the other's gesture, but thankfully we never addressed it.

As the years went on our relationship began to thaw, and we became peers with a lot of mutual respect for each other. We once did a show together at this fancy-schmancy tennis club, and we both absolutely killed it. Afterwards, he was so sweet and complimentary, and it meant the world to me that he liked my stand-up set. We were now members of our own mutual admiration society.

From then on, we would talk on the phone from time to time. He once threatened to do my podcast, and we planned to find a time that worked for both of us. Sadly, it never happened. I would learn that he had cancer. He was intensely private about it, and because we were not super-close with each other, I chose to never cross that line with him.

He died in 2015 at the age of 57. There was a service for him at the beach, and a laugh-out-loud hysterical memorial at The Comedy Store on Sunset; I went to both.

I have so many fond memories of our talks, but the one thing for which I will be eternally grateful to him is that in the late 1980's, he told me about this group called Young Artists United. It was an organization of some of the brightest young stars in Hollywood. People like Sarah Jessica Parker, Robert Downey, Jr., Esai Morales, Mary Elizabeth McDonough, Anne-Marie Johnson, Eric Stoltz, Sam Harris, and Daphne Zuniga were just some of the famous faces that you would see on any given week. And even Judd Nelson and Eve Plumb showed up from time to time, too.

It was started by actress Alexandra Paul, who starred in *Christine* and *Dragnet*, and also of *Baywatch* fame, along with producer Daniel Sladek. Daniel was one of the producers responsible for the movie version of

*Prayers for Bobby*, based on the true story of a boy who committed suicide due in part to his religious mother's disapproval of his homosexuality. Sigourney Weaver played Mary Griffith, Bobby's mother, in the film. It was also produced by Stanley M. Brooks, whose first A.F.I. film, *Epicac*, starred yours truly. The other producer of the film was Oscar-nominated David Permut... a friend of mine.

And I still couldn't get an audition!

Alexandra was the head of the new membership committee for Y.A.U., which is when I met her for the first time. I remember well my first impression of her; she was this beautiful goyisha (see: non-Jewish princess) actress from Connecticut. I was this awkward spiky-haired kook in a vintage sport coat, still trying to figure out who I was. We were both in our twenties, and on paper we could not have been more different, even in our careers. She was already a movie star, while I was a struggling young actor and comedian just trying to get a job. Yet from the moment we said, "Hello," she treated me as if I was an old friend. She made sure that I was comfortable and okay at the first meeting.

And our relationship blossomed from there. She started inviting me to various things, and all I could think was, 'Who is this person, and why is she asking to hang out with me? We have nothing in common!'

I have since come to realize that we have almost everything in common, even down to both of us having had an eating disorder. We are both very public about our struggles, sharing our stories by going to schools and talking about it. Our mutual pain and recovery and openness has been instrumental in us bonding as platonic soul mates. She is like the sister I never had.

Or rather... the one I always wanted; unfortunately, my biological sister never really worked out the way I had hoped.

Alexandra has loved me unconditionally, and knows more about me than anyone alive. She has shown me a different way to live, and taught me about the importance of giving back. She's an incredible environmentalist and an extraordinary political activist. She has even affected my shopping habits. Now whenever I buy something, I always think to myself, 'Do I really need this?' She has helped me realize that life isn't about things. Things will never make you happy. It's about the people, and it's about showing up for each other.

She has shown up for me like no other, and my life would have gone down a completely different path without her. She is the living true definition of friendship, even though she drives me crazy sometimes. She's intentional with her time, and God help you if you're trying to multitask while talking with her on the phone.

If only she had an Adam's apple, a prostate, and a penis! But I still love her with all my heart.

In the late 1990's, I met one of my best guy friends, Ernie Rhoads. He's a city-planner near Seattle, Washington, and an interior designer. We both attended a self-help conference called Focus at The Experience Workshop during the week before the New Year. He is one of the most hilarious people I've ever met… ten times funnier and smarter than I will ever be. He's also an incredible writer, and he always does what he says. He's a fabulous planner, especially for vacations.

Me? I'd be parked on my bed in my bathrobe, watching movies and eating room service, promising to get to the gym by this afternoon… oh look, *The Prince of Tides* is on TNT!

We first bonded with our sense of humor, and throughout that weekend we laughed so hard and made so many inappropriate jokes that Honey Ward – the leader of our "spiritual" retreat – thought of us as twelve-year-old boys and gave us a look that stated to all that we needed to be separated.

Ernie is gay, out, and somewhat divorced from a twenty-two-year relationship. He vacations with me, he holds my hand and gets me through my lowest points, and no matter what's going on, he always finds a way to bring the conversation back to him. He loves to tell the story about the time my dad took us both to lunch, and said he'd pay for our wedding.

"Dad," I laughed, "we don't like each other that way!"

I think that may have been the first time Lenny realized that not all gay people are attracted to each other. It slightly flummoxed him.

To sum up the difference between Ernie and myself: he loves to create drama in real life, and I like to keep it on the stage. I am the Yin to his Yang.

Ernie and I also have a distinct commonality that I share with Alexandra: we are all close to our mothers. In fact, I think my mother may love Ernie more than she loves me, which delights him to no end. She may love Alexandra more than me as well, virtually bonding with her through the magic of Alexandra's Lifetime movies. Gloria loves them even more than Alexandra's own mother.

I'll never forget the time that we introduced our mothers for the first time. They are both divorcees, and that's where the similarities end. Sarah was a therapist from England. Gloria was a beautician from Brooklyn. In other words, a perfect match.

Oy!

It was about twenty years ago, and we were at Alexandra's house. Sarah was telling this story about a hiking trip with a girlfriend in her wonderful English accent. My mom still smoked back then, so she kept zipping outside for a cigarette like a Russian spy. She only got about three-fifths of the story.

As Gloria raced back in for the crescendo of the tale, Sarah told us that her backpack was so heavy that she literally fell over.

"Backpack?" asked my mother, not fully grasping the entirety of the story. "I can't imagine having a backpack. How can you hike in heels with a backpack? I don't think I could do it holding my pocket book."

And with that, the room erupted in laughter... though not all of us knew whether my mother was kidding or not. Honestly, she was only half-kidding.

Of course, Gloria and Sarah were like conjoined twins compared to Ernie's mom, Cleo. Gloria had four husbands... two she married (literally) and two she killed (figuratively)… and is famous for wearing high heels to the beach. Ernie's mom was a bank teller who was married to the same man until he died. She also had the ability to take her bra off without removing her blouse when she got home from work… which is something I'll bet my mom could pull off with a little bit of training.

Maybe they aren't so different after all!

Friendship is such a subjective thing; everyone is in a different place during that first meeting, no matter where it is. When you are an actor and a comedian, you usually don't meet people next to you in a cubicle at the office. You have to reach out to them wherever you are, hoping that once you do make a friend, you have him or her for life.

Of course, you don't always know where that life is going to take you. Sometimes when you are friends with someone and their career takes off while you stay at your level, friendships don't always survive. It's always a wonderful surprise when they do.

I met Tiffany Haddish over twenty years ago at the Laugh Factory. I always knew that she was talented and funny, but who knew she would reach the stratospheric level she has? Oh yeah, she did… and I'm so proud of her! But being the classy gal that she is, she still returns my call or text, and she never makes me feel like I'm beneath her in any way. She is just so lovely.

And then other times, there are some people who just fade away… sometimes permanently, and others like waves in the ocean… leaving and returning on their own time. That's my friend, Anna Garduno. With her raspy voice and her larger-than-life personality, she instantly takes me back to the roots of my burgeoning acting career whenever we talk. She is also a total renaissance woman: an actor, a producer, a voice coach, and she gives me eternal hope as we grow older that new things are still possible.

Another one of my dearest friends is Sheila Kay, who has always been with me on the journey of my career. She is a legendary comedian who works a great deal on cruise ships, entertaining countless thousands of people every year. She can be just as happy working at sea and seeing the world while making people laugh, as she is relaxing at home at her house with her Republican Italian husband Robert in the woods in New Jersey. Yes, he's a Republican who likes gay people and believes in equal rights for all. Man, you never stop learning, and life has a way of keeping your heart open.

Sheila is like a big sister to me, as she's ten years older than I am. She has this way of enjoying life no matter what roadblocks fall into her path. Being in show business allows you to meet and work with people who you would never have the opportunity to in what would be considered a normal job, and I'm so thankful that our paths crossed all those years ago. She and her husband (who is gorgeous, by the way) are absolute family to me.

Sometimes you meet people who make you learn as much about yourself as you do about them. I met my friend, producer and actor Scott Crawford, in the late 1980's when he was starting a theater company in Los Angeles called The Dillon Street Players. I got to originate two roles for him in brand new plays. We even shared a role in one: *Biking with Andrew Scott* by Debbie Bolsky.

He's tall, eccentric, impatient, and incredibly caring. We had a lot in common, but in our early years of friendship, for some reason, I felt that there was always some unseen competition between us. In truth, he taught me that I sometimes needed to be more sensitive to others, when in reality, I had no idea there was something to which I needed to be sensitive.

One day we went to one of those cocktail parties that had a lot of gay men in show business. We were both single and looking for the one... while hoping to get a job at the same time. We got into an argument in the car on the way home. I don't know what we said, and the details never really matter, but when we stopped at a red light, he opened the door and jumped out.

I was stunned, and we didn't talk for a while.

Eventually, one of us broke down and called the other, saying we needed a little space. A few months after that he called me, we apologized to each other, and worked out some ground rules to our friendship. Thanks to that openness between Scott and myself, I gained some sensitivity I simply didn't have before, and learned one of the great lessons of my life.

If you stand in my apartment and look out at a particular spot from my window, you can see Bollea flowers growing on the railing of my terrace. If you stand in front of that same window but look in a different direction, you will see a piece of art by Joan Miró that my stepmother gave me after my father died. These are two utterly different perspectives while standing in the exact same place.

Sadly, things don't always work out that way. I had a friend I'll call Carrie. I met her through my friend Lydia Nicole, a wonderful actress and producer who I've been friends with since I was nineteen. She and another producer/actress friend, Luisa Leschin, got me involved in a group called Actors Rap Together, or A.R.T. The group disbanded, but we were always trying to recreate that model of talented people getting together, supporting each other, sharing information, and producing showcases. That's how I met Carrie.

She was an actress and comedian, and she had been very successful. She typically played nurses and people in law enforcement... but not the *Charlie's Angels* type. We would see each other as we had a lot of the same friends, and as the years went on, our lives seemed to become more intertwined. She once opened for me at a one-night gig that reminded me of playing the back room of a Denny's. I don't fully remember the gig, but I remember how I felt after it was over. There was this out-of-control funny element to her personality, but some of the reactions she displayed during certain situations were quite unexpected.

She was kind and generous, and yet, I had an innate fear of saying the wrong thing around her. Her moods went from trying too hard to completely shutting off, and there didn't seem to be a lot of middle ground. As much as I liked her, I could never get fully comfortable around her.

I remained a supportive friend to her during her times of need, including a bad break-up with a girlfriend. Yet even though she was out of the closet, she did not seem to be completely comfortable with it... and that sometimes translated to our relationship. There were times when I felt that she was uneasy with my not only being so publicly out, but such a passionate advocate for gay actors.

She would think that I didn't respect that she was bisexual, but to be honest, I could not have cared less who she loved as long as she was happy with her choice. But it was a mess of mixed signals, and while I had hope for getting through our differences like I was able to do with Scott, this didn't turn out the same way.

She essentially broke off our relationship over the phone, which was not my choice. I don't give up on friends easily. Maybe it's not always a bad thing; I'm still learning. We would still run into each other from time to time, but it was always awkward. Like so many times before, I was ready to put my head down and move forward.

But like almost everything in my life, once I make my mind up about anything, the universe intervenes and reminds me that I never know as much as I think I do. Just the other day, I walked into a restaurant with a young actor whom I mentor. One of the first faces I saw was Carrie, who was sitting at a table by herself eating lunch. We ended up getting a table beside her and having an absolutely lovely conversation during our meal.

Old dogs. New tricks. Thank you, Grandma Molly.

No matter how each one has ended up, I treasure the friendships that I've been gifted in my life. I've learned so much about myself, and how important it is to treat others the way I want to be treated. It has even prepared me for things yet to come... especially with my friend, David Hamilton.

I met David at a twelve-step meeting in 1999. He could not have been more different than me; he grew up the only son to a working class family in Worcester, Massachusetts. He is close to his sisters, his mother, and his aunts; his dad left his mother and her three children when David was just a toddler. He has a large family who love and care about him. They all seem to show up for each other, no matter what. They've even taken vacations together.

I can't even imagine! Vacationing together? Oh my God, my family couldn't make it through going out to lunch without someone starting World War III!

David was the guy who said "yes" to everything. He was very funny and always made fun of me for being in show business. He, himself, was a cable repairman. He used to say, "Well, if it's not on the front page of *Variety*, Jason won't understand it," as if I had to have the real world explained to me, which always made me laugh. He also never understood why going to see someone in a film or on stage meant so much to me. But, he showed up. He was like the brother I never had…

… and always wanted. Again, biology failed me.

Unfortunately, I don't know how much longer I'll have him, at least physically. He was diagnosed with two different cancers… one of them brain… and his time on the planet is more limited now. The cancer has changed him dramatically, both physically and emotionally, and now he's the guy who says "no" to a lot of things.

He lives right down the block from me. He sleeps a lot, and spends his waking hours playing with his two rabbits whom he adores. We talk on the phone, and I visit him whenever he's up for it. As hard as it is, it has given me the opportunity to show up for him in a way that is comfortable for him, but not always comfortable for me.

And that's okay because that's what friends do.

# 15

## Finding Me... Whoever That Is

So as I turned thirty, I once again wanted to lose that ten pounds that I'd been trying to shed since birth. I was on a diet before I could walk. I decided to go to an Overeaters Anonymous meeting to help kick-start my psyche, and my metabolism. I thought it was a diet club... but it was really so much more; I had no idea.

Weight was not the only thing on my mind. Thirty is such a milestone birthday in a person's life, and it was no different with me. I felt I was ready for some grand change... only I didn't know what it would be. After starting my twelve-step program for overeating, I also signed up for The Experience Workshop. It was an event to learn to accept who you were as a gay man, and how to be a leader while being powerful in that acceptance.

The workshop was started by David Goodstein and Dr. Rob Eichberg, and it was originally called The Advocate Experience. At that time, David was the owner of *The Advocate*, the most influential LGBTQ publication in the entire country... growing from a small local newspaper to a national magazine. In those early days, Goodstein and Eichberg personally facilitated the workshops.

I was told about the workshop by Jim Curtain, who I'd recently met... but I can't tell you where because it's anonymous! He was a mentor to me without him really knowing it. Jim also happened to be one of the managers for John Travolta… which was all I needed to know about him. If he was good enough for Travolta, he was good enough for me! He worked at a powerful management firm that I dreamed of being a part of… to no avail.

Jim also turned me on to a number of gay groups that really changed my life in how I participated in the community.

Being at the workshop really transformed me as a person. It was the first time I was actually able to talk about being gay in a public forum, and I was told that I had one of the longest "shares" at my orientation. My leader that weekend would become my guru in my life. Her name was Honey Ward, and she took over after all the original workshop creators had already passed away.

Honey was this powerful lesbian with a soothing, calming voice. I loved her khaki pants and blue Brooks Brothers button-downs with her short hair. She was kind, quick-witted, but no-nonsense. She was just who I needed at the time, even if I didn't think so. She really was the tough-love mother who I subconsciously craved, and she was one of the driving forces who showed me the way of how to be a man… or rather… a gay man.

The Experience Workshop had an amazing mission statement: By the year 2000, it will be absolutely okay to be lesbian or gay, and diversity will be valued and celebrated. This wasn't just a belief; it was a want… it was a need.

All of this was like being in a foreign land to me. I had been so busy hiding out in my closet that I never knew the world outside existed in this way. It was one of the most defining moments of my life, and it gave me the space I needed to eventually break through my proverbial closet door.

During the workshop, one of the things I had to do was write a letter to someone who harmed me. I wrote one to a guy named Jack, a former classmate. He never beat me up physically, but he verbally abused me all through junior-high and high school. We must have lived close to each other because I used to see him on the bus all the time; it was as if I couldn't escape his verbal hatred.

Of course, after writing him the letter in The Experience Workshop and letting him know how I felt, I had absolutely no idea I was going to have to mail it.

Yes, we actually mailed letters in those days, but it had been thirteen years since we were in high school together, so I didn't have his address. Thank God!

Sadly, I remembered that he knew Carole and Jack Shultz; Carole was an artist and Jack ran the business. I used to babysit their kids, Adam, Josh, and Rachel. Through them, I was finally able to track my tormentor down and give him a call. After a brief hello, I told him I was calling because I was supposed to reach out to people who gave me a hard time in school. He then told me that he had just gotten back from the hospital after trying to commit suicide.

Wow.

For a moment, I had no words. All I could think was that my bully now felt bullied by his own existence. It explained everything; this was a man who was in so much pain that he felt like he had to abuse me to keep from abusing himself. I had every intention of reading my letter to him, but I couldn't. I just listened to his story... and to his apology.

Sometimes, you don't need to tell people about the things they did to hurt you, especially if there is nothing they can do about it now. Sometimes, just to hear their voice and listen to their words is enough. Sometimes, your opinion doesn't need to be shared. This is what I learned from the twelve-step program.

Compassion.

I'm not sure what ever happened to Jack, but I wonder sometimes. I hope he's still with us, and has been able to move on from his pain.

In the feelings of sympathy that I had for Jack, I have come to realize that there has been a profound evolution in my being. It's a progression that I started with Overeaters Anonymous, and has organically grown into my journey with Al-Anon, even though I still go to an OA meeting from time to time. To me, Al-Anon is the master-class of the twelve-step program, and it encompasses all our vices and crutches. Food is my drug of choice, but Al-Anon teaches us that all our drugs of choice... food, sex, shopping, alcohol... are just the symptoms of our issues.

In Los Angeles, the recovery community is amazing, and for me, I've learned that Al-Anon is not always about having an alcoholic family member, lover, or friend; it's about accepting being powerless over the people, places, or things... and the alcoholic behavior, even if you don't drink. We call this being a dry drunk or an abusive person. And when I finally understood that, my life changed in such a big way.

Yes, I still struggle with weight, and yes I will always want to be ten pounds thinner, but the desire is no longer a need.

The willingness to look for self-discovery has impacted me in virtually every way. I now have a community, and most importantly, a means with which to communicate. I have this incredible structure and way of life that has allowed me to fire the office workers who lived in my head. And the president, who used to have a key to the executive washroom, now can't even get out of the parking garage. And many of his other cohorts have been relegated to the basement.

But when they slip up the back stairs to the penthouse, I now have the tools and the will to send them to the unemployment line. This program truly saved my life.

My journey from the early nineties through today has been very powerful for me. From starting to dip my toe into the world of being an openly gay person to being a passionate advocate for those who struggle with their sexuality and orientation, it has been an immensely meaningful metamorphosis. With the help of some really good therapists, the twelve-step program, The Experience Workshop, and the California Men's

Gathering (think of a camp for gay men without the booze or drugs), the work has led me down the road to become who I was always destined to be.

And I truly want to thank all the people who reached out to me, gave me a moment, listened to me talk way too much, and put up with my fear and insecurities. I would not be the man I am today without you.

# 16

## Burning Jason

As my search for self-awareness and acceptance continued, I was looking to expand my horizons and jump-start my creativity. It was 2010, and I was hosting a show on National Lampoon's Comedy Radio called *Sex.Com: We Do It On the Air*. It was co-hosted by an ex-porn star, and all we talked about was sex and dating and relationships. It was a difficult show to host, as once again I was working with people who had never worked in comedy before, but thought they knew everything. They never wanted to plan anything, and thought they could just wing it.

Oy!

My friends knew I was stuck in a rut, and an inordinate number of them kept telling me that I might find my creative spark at Burning Man. However, they also told me that I shouldn't go by myself for my first foray. I had met an artist named Michael Bonfiglio at the California Men's Gathering, and I had this major crush on him. Sadly, he just wanted to be my friend and not my lover, though it didn't stop my visceral reaction to him. He had this sweet and sexy kind of goofiness that was intoxicating.

While he wouldn't share his bed with me, he was sweet enough to connect me with a group called the Astro-Pups. He explained that this was a group of gay men who liked to wear dog costumes made out of fake fur.

No, I'm not kidding.

The lead pup... let's call him 'John'... owned a health food business. He also did daddy bear-porn on the side... not that there's anything wrong with that.

During a 'get to know you' session on the phone, I was introduced to many of the other members, most of whom lived in San Francisco. I very much wanted to learn how to be a part of their group... to not be somebody different. Like so often in my life, I just wanted to be one of the guys, which has always been sort of hard for me.

So using only my first name, the moment, "Nice to meet you," left my lips, one of the guys jumped in and said, "Oh, you sound just like that comedian Jason Stuart. I love him!"

"Well thank you," I said. "I'm him."

"You're not!"

"I am!"

"No! Really!"

And... there went the idea of me being just one of the guys.

Since I already stuck out by what I did for a living, and by the sheer fact that I didn't spend my weekends dressed up like a Basset Hound, I wanted to do everything I could to blend in with these guys. So after months of planning, I began shopping for all the equipment I knew I would need for Burning Man.

I was told that when you first arrive, you learn quickly that there is a playa with porta-potties... and not much else. So I bought a tent, a camel-back backpack for water, a sleeping bag, and all the necessary accoutrements that I thought I might need to have. I also made sure nothing was extra-fancy or ostentatious so that I wouldn't come across like an out-of-touch actor. I even brought my best friend David's used folding chair.

The day before we were supposed to arrive, I packed up my white two-door classic Toyota RAV4 and drove to San Francisco. I arrived at Johnny Healthy Porn's house to spend the night before departing with the rest of the Astro-Pups the next day. He had a long-haired cat, and damned if it didn't feel like every one of those hairs seemed to permeate every orifice in my face. My sinuses exploded with what can only be described as a violent allergic reaction.

When I woke up the next morning, I mainlined as much Allegra as was legal. This was potentially the first clue that things weren't going to go well.

Two weeks prior, the porn-star/health-food store owner said that I could grab a bunk in the camper that we were taking down to Burning Man. Now, he was rescinding that offer so that he could use it as a twenty-four-hour sex club should he get lucky. This wasn't even the camper we were supposed to have. Originally he had a line on a larger one, but that fell through. Now we had an under-sized shit-box that I no longer had access to besides the ride to and fro.

So there we were... me, the porn-star, Hard-of-Hearing Benny (who was a bit older than all of us), and a few younger guys. If it wasn't bad enough, this thing had the pick-up of a hamster on a treadmill. It would only go forty-five miles an hour, and that's while going downhill with a tailwind while stroking the shifter and talking dirty to it.

As we pulled into the venue, we made a plan: the younger puppies would fill every empty container we had at the water tanks, while we went to claim our spot. We pulled up to our patch of land and parked the sub-recreational sex-wagon, which was also pulling a U-Haul trailer full of food and water that we'd bought before we left.

Now keep in mind... it's now 10 pm, and my entire diet for that day consisted of a Starbuck's breakfast sandwich at about 7 am, a bag of nuts and raisins for the road, and a Diet Coke (which I no longer drink). We had yet to unload any of the food from the trailer, and I was beyond starving. While waiting for the younger crew to return, the porn-star brought out a tin of pot cookies. I downed four of them before he had the chance to tell me I shouldn't. I like cookies.

What! I couldn't help it!

Apparently, I over-did the recommended intake by approximately eight hundred percent. The sweats gave way to fear, which gave way to so much paranoia that I refused to set up my tent; I was afraid that I would completely screw it up, and I wanted my part of the campsite to look pretty!

After the younger guys came back with the water, they arranged their tents in a horseshoe pattern. My tent mimicked my place in the universe… off to the side and not attached to anything. Like Pluto, which isn't even considered a planet anymore.

After I completed my set-up with the porn-star's help, I stood back to look at my work, and I couldn't stop anything from spinning like a whirlpool inside a kaleidoscope.

And then I passed out.

The next morning, I woke up to a sandstorm that enveloped the entire campground. I barely had time to wipe the spittle from my mouth before all of us took shelter in one of the larger tents. For six hours, it felt like being in the middle of Hurricane Katrina. Only with sand. Of course, the porn-star wouldn't let any of us into the camper; he was still sleeping and the door was locked. So here I was sitting on a bench next to a bunch of guys dressed up like stuffed animals. I will say that the commitment to their craft was impressive.

After the storm subsided, I toured the playa where I found the most outrageous art around every turn. Some of it was so detailed and bursting with talent, and some… just wasn't. A few looked like a five-year-old made them in kindergarten, and got a 'D' just for the lack of effort.

And for some reason, I wasn't able to connect with the Astro-Pups… surprise, surprise. They were all gay and living out loud with their passions; why couldn't I break through their barrier? As it turns out, their barrier was that they were all on LSD!

Soooooo… that explains it!

Thankfully, LSD was not my problem. The pot cookies, however, were. I must have ingested enough to choke an elephant because twenty-four hours after downing them, I was still high as a freaking kite and completely paranoid. I had to get a change of scenery before I went out of my mind, so I grabbed my camel-back full of water and headed to the center of the grounds. There were enough things making me uncomfortable here... I didn't need dehydration to be one of them. The aridity of the air made it necessary.

Only I wasn't getting all the water my camel-back could hold. Sadly mine leaked, and no one bothered to tell me about it. So without actually realizing it, and without getting my full hydration, the leaking water made it look like I was continually peeing on myself for my entire time at Burning Man.

Later that night I met this wonderful man who I thought I was in love with. I thought he was definitely the one. Yet to this day, because I was so damn high from those effing pot cookies, I don't know whether I actually met him, or imagined him.

The next day I awoke in my little tent... still off to the side. Now that the sandstorm was over, I could see that the horseshoe tents were all palaces compared to my tiny little bungalow. Apparently, I was the only one who was roughing it. They all had state-of-the-art tents that you could actually walk into without ducking and stand up tall once inside.

And there was mine... barely big enough to house my sleeping bag... all because I didn't want to look like a diva actor. There goes trying to fit in.

Again.

I also failed to remember that civilized humans sleep on mattresses, even when bunking in a tent. As I had neglected to purchase an air-mattress, my back went completely out. I rolled out of my abode and I hobbled to the food in the U-Haul to make myself a bowl of cereal.

I was still high, by the way. Damn cookies.

After I walked into the trailer to assemble my breakfast, one of the Astro-Pups rolled the trailer door down a bit to keep the desert air from getting to the food. Of course, I didn't actually notice this at the time as I was still high! So while walking and eating, and not paying attention to my new spatial reality, and still rather out of it, I banged my head on the bottom edge of the door.

And then I passed out.

When I came to, all the other guys were gone. Disoriented, and possibly desperate and definitely alone, I tried looking for my "boyfriend" from the night before, to no avail. As I wandered around, I found a twelve-step meeting in the middle of the chaos. After a while I found myself at another location where I sat watching, and eventually dancing, with a lot of naked people who really should have kept their clothes on.

It was now the fourth day of the seven that I had committed to, but I was done. The thought of seventy-two more hours felt like torture, and this Jew had already had enough torture in his life. So I wandered around to the center of the camp to look for a way out. I found a gal in the information center with one of her boobs sticking out of her blouse. At first I thought it was an old tan handbag. She said that there was a bus that would take me to a little town about ten miles away from where we were that had a hotel, a gas station, and a general store. From there, I could either find another bus, or I could hitchhike. Both sounded less than ideal, but at least it was an escape from the stuffed animals in this land of misfit toys.

After she gave me rough directions to the bus stop, I went back to camp, left a note for the porn-star (who was out looking for sex with his pack of canine minions), loaded up my roller suitcase with all it could carry (yeah, I was that guy), and I got the hell out of dodge… without my tiny tent or my friend David's used folding chair. I felt bad about leaving the chair (he still teases me about it), but with the roller, my duffle bag on my back, and a small cooler full of provisions that I stole from the trailer, I literally couldn't carry anything else. I set out on my mile-long journey to the bus stop.

At Burning Man they have these vehicles called Art Cars, and they're decorated to look like all sorts of things. I saw one cruise by that looked like a flying carpet. I flagged it down like I was hailing a cab in New York City, and asked the driver if he'd take me to the bus stop. He let me put my luggage on the carpet, but he said he wasn't comfortable with me being a passenger. To this day, I have no idea why he wouldn't let me in the fucking car… like I was the weird one!

So I followed this Aladdin wannabe on foot. After about a half-mile, something felt off.

"Hey, do you know where you are going?" I yelled.

"I'm just driving!" he called back.

What?!

"Hey, can you take me to the bus stop?" I inquired.

"I'm not sure!" he said.

"Why?" I barked.

"I don't know where I'm going!" he responded. Apparently, his level of commitment was that vague. It seems everyone had access to that tin of pot cookies.

"Are you kidding me?" I yelled.

"No, I'm not!" he replied.

Oy!

Miraculously, we finally found our way to the bus stop, but no one was there. While waiting, I struck up a conversation with a guy who said he could drive me to Sacramento when his car got back.

"That's terrific!" I said. "When is your car supposed to be back?"

"Yesterday."

As the wait continued, I met this twenty-year-old red-headed Philip Seymour-Hoffman-look-alike sitting on a bench. He lamented to me that he came to Burning Man to lose his virginity, but he couldn't find a girl to do it with him. How sad… in every way imaginable. I told him to never stop trying, to prevail, and that it would eventually happen.

Two hours later my ride finally showed up. It looked like the school bus from *The Partridge Family* mated with a station wagon from the seventies, with wood paneling on the sides. Inside, there was this young

Asian guy snagging a ride out of there as well. He said he was straight, but he wanted to kiss me.

Calgon, take me away!

It was a forty-five-minute ride to the little town, and the first half of it was spent letting down the straight boy who wanted to kiss me. The rest of the time, I made a sign that read, "Need to get to San Francisco. Will pay for gas."

After we arrived at the little town and I got off the bus, I held up my sign. It was my first hitchhike in decades, but I was desperate; I just wanted to go home. Just like a Doris Day movie, not two minutes after my feet hit the ground, a truck pulled up and I heard some kid yell, "That's Dr. Thomas!"

It was like being in a movie on Lifetime!

An uncle and his nephew were headed to Sacramento. The kid had seen me in one of my most popular roles on the sitcom *My Wife & Kids...* more on that later. Suffice it to say, he was a big fan. I got in their truck, still dumbfounded by my luck. It was the easiest hitchhike of my life!

After we pulled into Sacramento they took me for Thai food, and then brought me back to the uncle's apartment where I took a shower. I hadn't realized just how much dirt covered my body. By the time I was finished, you could have made a sand castle with what I left in their tub.

My flip-phone was partially waterlogged, so the screen had stopped working. Thankfully, the numbers on the keypad were still functional. I called the airlines, but there were no flights to San Francisco to be had. In yet another example of extreme kindness, this nice man and his nephew drove me to the Greyhound bus station where I was able to get a ticket back to my car in the porn-star's driveway, where it was parked.

As I waited, I sat next to a soldier who told me that he was going home to his wife, which made me happy. Then he said that he would go back for another tour to make more money for him and his wife to buy a home, which made me sad.

I told him, "No, you'll get your penis shot off!"

'Who is this nutcase?' he must have thought.

"Things are crazy over there. There's no guarantee you'll come home alive if you go back. Get a safer job so that you can go home to your wife!"

By the time we ended our conversation, he told me he wasn't going to go back, which thrilled me. One more kid not getting shot.

I also ran into a comedian who I had worked with twenty years prior. He used to want to date my sister, and he asked how she was.

"Orthodox," I said. "A lot of good you did! Thanks for nothing!"

I was only slightly kidding.

After I got on the bus and settled in, I ended up sitting behind this woman named Leticia. She had the most outrageous hairstyle, leggings, high-top shoes, and an oversized shirt that read, "I'm Juicy."

I'll bet!

"Where are you going?" she asked.

"Going back to San Fran to get my car," I replied. "Where are you going?"

"Me and my husband got arrested for having weed in our car. I just got bailed out."

"Where's your husband?"

"He hasn't gotten bailed out yet."

"You left him in jail? Why?"

"I have to go home and pay my bills."

"In person?!"

"I always have to pay my bills in person!"

Dear. God.

But the saddest part of the ride to San Francisco was the family from Kansas City. They were headed north to Seattle to look for work. They had both recently been laid off, and they were desperate for a fresh start. They had four children, all under the age of ten. The youngest was a baby. The six of them had been making the journey by car, but while staying at a cheap motel, it was stolen along with most of what they owned in the world. It broke my heart.

The bus driver pulled over at a rest stop so that we could stretch our legs, pee, and grab a snack. As we got off the bus, Leticia said to me, "If you get me some Spicy Doritos and a Mountain Dew, I'll make sure that nobody rapes you."

Now, how could I pass up an offer like that?

I then looked over at the family and couldn't bear to see them with nothing, so I bought them chips and drinks, too. I brought them over, and the mom was so thankful. As Leticia and I stood to the side watching the children hungrily gobble up their snacks, an ash from the mother's cigarette flew off and landed on top of her six-year-old's head. Leticia reacted quickly… worried that the poor kid's hair would catch fire at any second. So she casually walked over and poured a splash of Mountain Dew onto the ash so that he wouldn't go up in flames. I was the only one who noticed, and it took every ounce of restraint I had to keep from bursting out laughing.

Back on the bus for the last leg, there was a sweet old drunk man in the back singing, "Come to the Florida Sunshine Tree." At that moment, that's exactly where I wanted to be.

At 5 am, we finally pulled into San Francisco. I leaped off the bus and straight into a cab driven by a Russian who couldn't speak a word of English; I have no idea how he found his way to my car at the porn-star's house. After paying the man, I dug my key out of my bag and opened my car door. I don't think I'd been this happy to get behind the wheel since the day I got my license.

I drove to a hotel where I'd made a reservation on my non-screen-working phone. After checking in, I flopped onto the bed and turned on the television, only to discover *The Prince of Tides* starring… yes… Barbra Streisand. And it was just starting! I spent two hours crying like a baby.

Oh… Barbra… you're always there for me!

And then I passed out.

The next morning I woke up and took a shower, leaving another sand castle in the tub. After toweling off and getting into some comfortable clothes, I checked out, got into my white two-door classic Toyota RAV4, and drove back to Los Angeles.

Burning Man was now checked off my bucket list... forever. Unless, of course, Jon Hamm wants to whisk me back there in his mobile home. But I'm not holding my breath.

# 17

# You Call That Acting?

In 2006 I wanted to tape my own stand-up comedy special. No one was doing that at that time. You had to get a deal with HBO, Showtime, or Comedy Central, and none of them was banging down my door. I had the wherewithal to be a futurist and see that this was the way to go to further my career. And furthering that career meant making my own special.

And these days, everyone makes their own comedy special. I guess I'm a trailblazer of sorts.

I decided to call it *Making it to the Middle*. It made sense to me; I was in the middle of my life, the middle of my career, and I was mostly working in the middle of the country. I also wanted the special to be shot in a comedy club so as to represent my experience of where I came from, and how all this material was created.

I have a filmmaker friend named Lisa Sanow who is incredibly talented and organized, and I asked her if she would help me to produce and direct it. Thank God she said yes because without her, I could never have done it.

I had booked a gig to headline The Funny Bone Comedy Club in Columbus, Ohio. I thought this was the perfect place to tape it. We would use four shows with a three-camera setup… two on Friday and two on Saturday. After recording, I would pick the show I liked best, and would use that as the backbone, and then fill in the gaps with clips from the other shows.

I wore the same thing, wore my hair the same way, and used similar camera angles each night. Of course, this is when I actually had hair.

I sold the special to Here TV, which was the first gay pay-per-view network. I sold the DVD rights to Ariztical Entertainment, and they, in turn, sold it to Netflix. The special cost me $10,000, but I doubled it in profits. Honestly, I'm still making money on it.

It was on Netflix before anyone and everyone had a show on Netflix, and as of writing this, Here TV has re-upped with me, so it's going to keep showing on all their platforms for the foreseeable future.

I was very proud of the fact that I had a special that culminated my work as a nightclub comedian. However, after this incredible experience, things seemed to change. I hit a creative wall, and I was unsure of what to do next.

So I waited for a sign. I got a gig at Zanies Comedy Night Club in Chicago, where they forgot to pick me up at the airport and they took me to the wrong hotel. It was one of their coldest winters yet. Almost all my radio and TV interviews were cancelled because of the snow... even the one with Danny Bonaduce, which was my favorite.

After one of the nights at the comedy club, I had a promotional night at a local gay club where I could sell my DVDs and sign autographs. They put me in a dark corner with a table as the music played really loudly and the lights went on and off. And I remember one guy said, "Isn't that Jason Stuart? What's he doing standing in a corner all by himself?"

Everything that could go wrong... did. I felt like Jennifer Grey when Patrick Swayze said, "Nobody puts Baby in the corner!"

I was tired, I was getting older, and I wanted to be more creative, but I didn't know exactly what to do. So I sat down and had a conversation with myself (which I do a lot) and said, "What do I really want?"

I enjoy doing so many things, but if I had to choose one love of my life, it would be acting... even though at that time I was more well-known for being a comedian. It reminds me so much of Barbra Streisand who always saw herself as an actress first, or Shirley MacLaine who always saw herself as a dancer first; being in front of the camera and becoming someone else will always hold my heart like nothing else.

So I decided to go back to acting class, emphasizing working on my voice. I wanted to work on lowering it, so that I could play different characters, even older people... creating a depth in my work with more purpose.

Of course, playing an older person wasn't going to be too much of a stretch because, dear God, I was becoming an older person!

I studied with several different acting coaches over the years. The ones who really made an impression on me were Roy London... who taught me how to go after things and play action in a scene, and Ivana Chubbuck.... who taught me how to focus and block out all the noise in my head, which, to me, is one of the most important things in acting. She offered me respect, which gave me tremendous confidence that I had not had before.

And then I started studying with another one of the masters, Larry Moss... who taught me to stand my ground, to not be afraid of my power, and how to use my presence on stage. Larry was a culmination of the evolution that began in my twenties, when I studied with Nina Foch who taught me to always come from some place, and always go to some place.

During the late 90's and early 2000's, I did a lot of sitcoms. My comedian friend, Drew Carey, gave me my first guest starring role... starting my career of playing managers. I was the manager of the appliance department where Drew worked. Kate Walsh played his girlfriend in a fat suit. I was to instruct people in this contest, using appliances as if they were part of an Olympic sport.

I was even replacing an actor who got fired, so I knew this was a rare opportunity, and I wanted to make Drew proud of me, to show my appreciation by doing a great job. But I just didn't understand the episode.

What I learned was that the producers didn't understand it either. Nor the writers. In fact, no one was happy with the script. Even the appliances they were going to use weren't able to work and made no sense in the scene.

They needed to re-write it, and fast. I thought that I was stupid and didn't understand what was going on, and that's when I figured out that I was dyslexic.

I had seen Tom Cruise on a morning show once, and he talked about how he would sometimes get confused by switching words around. But I'm not Tom Cruise, so I was too afraid to ask questions. So I called my good friend Jacquie Mendenhall, and spent the whole weekend with her drilling me, so that I would know my lines backwards and forwards by my call time on Monday.

I'd never been on a sitcom in front of a live audience before, and I didn't want anyone to know. I wanted to give the impression that I was perfect. But with a script that I didn't understand, and no experience to pull it off, how the hell would I come up with perfect?

And when you're dyslexic and you learn everything by rote, your perspective is skewed. I thought that I was in a no-win situation, and I was within an inch of quitting.

Thankfully, the network gods were smiling down on me. The writers worked feverishly to come up with a new and much better script... one that everyone could understand. Apparently, I was not alone in my confusion, and realizing that I wasn't crazy gave me a jolt of confidence that I really needed.

We were to shoot on Monday, and Jacquie worked with me until I had my breakthrough: I found out how to play the part. This was the beginning of me starring in a string of situation comedies.

I did two episodes of *Will & Grace*, where I played "Stuart," the manager of the duplex where Sean Hayes' character did his show Just-Jack! They changed the script so many times on that show that I went from having a guest starring role in both episodes, to half a line in one, and being completely cut out of the other. Glenn Close guest-starred in the latter episode. I saw her off to the side, sitting with her script in hand, and I think she said to me, "I've been nominated for an Academy Award four times; I can't do this." At least that's what I think she said.

Being on *Will & Grace* was like being on *Survivor*... you never knew when you were going to get voted off. But I have to tell you that I'm very thankful that I got to be in this iconic show. It's a credit I'm very proud of, and I can't thank my producer friend Jhoni Marchinko enough for getting me the interview, and my comedy pal Louie Anderson for introducing me to her. It's true what they say: everything in Hollywood is six degrees of separation.

I worked on an episode of *Norm*, starring comedian Norm Macdonald... who I'd met years ago while headlining a comedy club in Canada, Laurie Metcalf from *Roseanne*, and Faith Ford from *Murphy Brown*. TV royalty. I had one scene that morphed into two. I never left the set... I just sat there and watched these television icons work their craft. It was like watching a TV sitcom master class.

More sitcoms and TV dramas followed, most of them forgettable... save for an episode of *Charmed*, where I played... shocker... a manager of the restaurant "Quaked" where Piper, played by Holly Marie Combs, worked. I fashioned myself as the Larry Tate character from *Bewitched*... when she would put a spell on Larry, and he never knew what hit him.

I had a scene with Shannen Doherty and Alyssa Milano, both so beautiful, young, and successful. It was my first experience of watching twenty-somethings on their phones most of the time... flip-phones, no less. I thought, 'God, this is weird.'

All of this brought me to my big break of getting the recurring role of "Dr. Steven Michael Thomas" on *My Wife & Kids*.

I was doing a one-nighter at The Russian River, a gay resort near San Francisco, when I got a call from my agent who said, "They want you to do *My Wife & Kids*." It was a hugely popular show on ABC starring my old comedy pal Damon Wayans, and Tisha Campbell from the show *Martin*.

As the story was told back to me, in the writers' room, they wrote the part of a gay marriage counsellor. The people in the room were producer Don Reo who had cast me in *The John Larroquette Show*, Damon – the star, Jim Vallely from *Arrested Development*, and my pal comedian Bruce Fine – all writer-producers on the show, and comedians who I'd worked with in the past. When they saw the character and talked about who should play the role, word has it that everyone said my name. It was a divine intervention of perfect comedic timing. Sometimes, things just have your name on it.

In those days, we would do a 5:30 pm taping, and a 7:30 pm taping. We would do the show as written, and then Damon would do some improvising around the lines. He told me I could do the same, which opened up a Pandora's Box that I'm not sure he was ready for. I don't think he knew how much I love to improvise. I've always felt like it was my ace in the hole.

You can see during that first episode that it's not the characters laughing at my jokes… it's Damon and Tisha's pure reaction to what they were hearing. The audience loved me and the network loved me, as did the producers, the writers, and actors; it was a dream come true. Everything fell into place. I was asked back to do another episode, and then another one after that.

But something was off in those later episodes… something that was out of my control. I was told that Damon did not like his character going to therapy. He felt it made him look weak. I don't know whether that was the truth or a work of fiction, but those are the things that were told to me through other showbiz friends and my manager at the time.

But it was undeniable that this handful of episodes of *My Wife & Kids* changed my career… and changed me. It moved me to the next place that I needed to be as an actor, and for that, I'm forever grateful to Damon, Don, Jim, Bruce, and so many of the writers on the show.

And I especially want to thank Kim Wayans and Janis Hirsch, who wrote episodes specifically for me, and my favorite sitcom TV director

James Widdoes… the man who played Robert Hoover in *Animal House*. He was one of those guys who made you feel like you could do your best work all the time.

So after years of being on the road, I decided that I would focus on my acting career, and I would only do stand-alone dates for comedy. In 2009, I guest-starred on an episode of *The Closer*, produced and written by my friend Adam Belanoff. I played a… drum roll please… manager of a storage facility who found a dead body in a large Styrofoam cooler. They were having trouble finding the right guy for this role. All the potential actors were white, paunchy, straight guys. I decided to play him like a neurotic New York Jew, very much like a lot of the people I grew up with.

The creator of the show, James Duff, loved it and I was cast. I got to work with the brilliant Kyra Sedgwick and the veteran character actor G. W. Bailey of *Police Academy* fame. This started the next phase of my career: playing annoying Jews. Working with Kyra was pure joy. She was so present, and it really left an impression on me and changed the way I work now. She seemed to have this ability to stop everything going on around her to focus on the job at hand.

So after that, with each new role, I became more focused and more specific about my work.

A few years prior, I got two different supporting roles in two different films that I did back-to-back. In *Coffee Date*, I got to play an office manager who thought his co-worker was gay. I worked my craft to make each scene different, and to make each moment as specific as possible… hoping for happy accidents to come through the lens. In every scene, I had to talk about how my character was sure that my co-worker was gay. I figured out a way to do it differently in each scene… except one where I ordered food at a Chinese restaurant.

I could not figure out how to make this scene unique, until I sat down and picked up the menu. So the director, Stewart Wade, let me improvise all the funny names of Chinese food. That kept my head in the menu the whole time. Hence, I found another creative way to play the scene by using the props at my disposal. And when the film was released, people took notice of my work as an actor, not only a comedian.

The other film was a pot-smoking comedy called *Puff, Puff, Pass*, where I played… you guessed it… a manager… this time of a rehab center. We all thought *Puff, Puff, Pass* was going to be a major hit (no pun intended) through Sony pictures, due to the pedigree of the cast, which included some of the funniest actors in the biz, including Terry Crews from *Brooklyn Nine-Nine*, LaVan Davis from *House of Payne*, Constance Marie from *George Lopez*, Jonathan Banks from *Breaking Bad*, John C. McGinley from *Scrubs*, Darrel Hammond from *Saturday Night Live*, David Faustino from *Married with Children*, Kevin Nealon from *Weeds*, Mo Collins from *Fear the Walking Dead*, and Jaleel White from *Family Matters*… just to name a few. OMG!

You never know what's going to happen to a film. It was the directing debut of Mekhi Phifer, famous for his work on *ER*. On paper, this was going to be a massive success in the theatres. However, it never got the chance: it went straight to DVD, where it has since become a cult hit. One day I was walking down the street in Hollywood after a date at an art gallery show. Some guy who looked homeless came over to me, and my date said, "Ooh, let's walk in the other direction."

"Hey," the homeless-looking guy said, "*Puff, Puff, Pass*, man!"

"Don't worry," I said, "he knows me from my pot movie."

"So funny, man!" he continued. "You got a joint?"

All I could do was laugh. And now whenever it happens… and it happens more than I ever thought it would… I know it's because of that movie.

My career was in full swing. Each role brought me to the next. I risked, I studied, and I worked hard. I read everything I could get my hands on to find out who was casting what, and where. I sent notes, emails, and links of my work to everyone I could. I kept my nose to the grindstone, and in the process, I was able to turn my career from a funny gay comedian to a funny sitcom guy, to prolific character actor… not having any family members in show business, and not having an agent or a manager who held my hand. It was all just by pure tenacity.

Sometimes my father would tease me about a job. I called him once and said, "Dad, I just got a guest spot on a show calls *Everybody Hates Chris*."

He said, "Vy do you have to be on a show that everybody hates? Vy can't you be on *Everybody Loves Raymond*? I mean, they love Raymond. They hate Chris. Vy can't you be on the show where they love the guy? I hate that show. I'll pay for you not to be on that show."

Over the years, I've had guest spots on some really high-profile shows like *House* opposite Hugh Laurie, and *It's Always Sunny in Philadelphia* with the brilliantly funny Danny DeVito, who I'd actually met as a teenager. At that time he was living in the maid's room of Joe Santos' house, who played Dennis Becker on *The Rockford Files*. His son, Joey Santos, Jr., was my buddy in high school. Danny was dating the woman who became his wife, actress Rhea Perlman, and she confided in me that she thought she would never make it as an actress in Hollywood, as no one would hire someone who looked like her to be on a series.

Of course a few years later, she would get cast in the history-making *Cheers*.

I also got to work with the comedy genius Judd Apatow on his show *Love*, where I played a shrink, again. And I had a genuinely lovely experience acting with Keanu Reeves and Peter Stormare in the hilarious show *Swedish Dicks*, where I played a Mafioso congressman named Oscar Bustemente. I had no idea I was half-Cuban until I got on the show.

But you never know what job is going to take you where. I kept plugging away, until I guested on a little show called *Warren the Ape*, which was a companion series to *Greg the Bunny*. It was directed by the brilliant Sean Baker, who also co-wrote it with his talented writing partner Chris Bergoch. It was another show where I got to improvise a lot while playing a Bernie Madoff-type character who shares a prison cell with a talking puppet.

Yes, you read that right. My first human-to-puppet acting, with puppeteer and *Robot Chicken* voice-actor, Dan Milano.

And Dr. Drew Pinsky played his shrink. Really.

Before I went to set, I did my due diligence and discovered that Sean had directed one of my favorite indie films, *Prince of Broadway*. After wrapping the TV show, we stayed in touch, verbally and by text. Meeting in person though, was another matter. He was wonderful, but insanely busy.

A year after that, I acted in another wonderful indie film called *Love is Strange*, where I played the wedding officiant and friend of these two older gay men, played by John Lithgow and Alfred Molina. I had a three-page scene where I was the only one who spoke... except when the couple says, "I do."

Needless to say, I was a nervous wreck. Every actor on the set had either been nominated, or had actually won, a Tony, an Emmy, or an Oscar. They included Marisa Tomei, Harriet Harris, and Cheyenne Jackson, to name a few. The thing I really learned is that the more successful people really are, the more gracious they are to work with... ninety-nine percent of the time.

And FYI, I'd been writing to the director of *Love is Strange*, Ira Sachs, for years... hoping to work with him, but it didn't happen until my pal Jim Lande, the producer of another film I did called *BearCity 2: The Proposal*, got me a script. I read through *Love is Strange* ferociously, and was so touched by it. The part wasn't even a want, it was a need... something that I felt I didn't want to live without.

I found a few roles in the script that I was right for, and I was asked to put an audition tape together for Avy Kaufman, one of the most prestigious casting directors out of New York. If it had not been for Jim, I never would have gotten that opportunity, so thanks, Jim! Of course, I never would have met Jim if I hadn't met the man who introduced us, Doug Langway, who I'd met at Outfest, an LGBTQ film festival.

Six degrees, people. See how it works? This stuff doesn't just happen by chance.

*Love is Strange* was the first in my trifecta of Sundance films. Next was *Tangerine*, the film that was shot on an iPhone so brilliantly, about a day in the life of two transgender gals. That film literally fell into my lap. I got a call from Sean Baker's producer, Darren Dean, asking if I would be interested in playing the character of "Joey the Doorman." They wanted me to read the pages and consider the role.

"Is Sean Baker the director?" I asked.

"Yes."

"I'm in!"

"Don't you want to read it?" Darren asked.

"Sure," I said. "But I'm in!"

These roles prepared me for the final film of my trifecta, and the role that would change me irreversibly to my soul. It would be the proudest moment of my professional career.

Sadly, someone close to my heart wouldn't be there to see it.

# 18

## Two Down, One Up

He survived the Holocaust. He survived the boat to the New World. He survived learning the English language... no small feat. He survived New York, Los Angeles, and everywhere in between. He even survived being married to my mother. But in 2012, cancer caught up to my father, Lenny Greif.

This once strapping and powerful man had become a physical shell of himself. My stepmother Linda and my brother Steve had rented a hospital bed that stayed in the middle of his bedroom so that he wouldn't have to move around so much. He was so weak, and everyone knew we didn't have a lot of time left. I called my stepmother every day and told her I was coming by, though she would always say, "He's sleeping and very weak, so there's no need to come."

Like that was going to keep me away.

I frequently dropped by the house they'd lived in since the 1980's, just to get as many moments as I could while I still had time. I felt a quiet hush every time I walked through the front door. Usually, it was Linda and Steve who would be there, as Steve had now taken over the reigns of my father's work, and really life... much like I did for my grandmother Molly before she died.

My brother was deeply affected by my father's illness, as all of us were. He and our stepmother seemed to draw into themselves, enduring their intense, silent pain. I would never be allowed to hear it, but it was so marked on their faces. It was just so loud... a thunderous silence.

My dad and I would have this instant connection whenever we were together. He would lie in his bed and we would talk. On one of his last days, I yearned to be closer to him, so I laid down next to him.

"When I was fourteen, you took me on my first plane ride to San Francisco," I said. "Why did you take me and not my brother and sister?"

He simply said, "Because you needed it."

It was one of the single-most generous things he ever did for me.

He just had a way of being present for you, and you alone. I think it's partly because he seemed to have separate relationships with everyone. To me, everything appeared disjointed and compartmentalized, but it made sense to him. He was able to make a person the center of his universe at any given moment, and I lived for those moments when I was that center.

As the end drew nearer, my brother called to tell me that our father was getting much weaker. Steve had no idea, but I already knew; my dad and I had been speaking on the phone regularly, and I could hear his voice fading.

A few days before he died, I stopped by to find a house full of people: my brother and his wife Terri, my niece Heather, my aunt Micki and uncle Mike, my step-brother Jeff, and my sister. They were all hanging out in the kitchen. As I walked into the house, I passed them while offering a reciprocated quick hello or a nod.

I walked past the kitchen and into the den, thinking that my dad might be in there watching television. Instead, I found my sister's husband Ronnie and their four children. He had a devious smirk on his face, like some sort of cat had finally been let out of the bag. I'd never met the children before, so the moment was shocking to say the least.

Everyone knew that I wasn't allowed to have any relationship with my sister's children, but not one person in that kitchen gave me a heads-up as to what I was walking into. No one said anything.

Not a word.

I felt this wash of emotion go across my entire being. It felt like I'd been thrown into a cold bath of water. As I stood in the room while they all sat on the couch and in chairs, I remember saying, "I guess I'm the best kept secret."

I went around the room, pretending to correctly guess each of their names to their faces, all the while trying not to completely break down. I didn't want to make a scene or to make this moment about me. To be honest, I didn't even want to be there anymore. After the unpleasant pleasantries, I excused myself to the kitchen. I asked my sister, "How did you want me to handle this?" She seemed to have no understanding of what I was going through.

"There's nothing to do," she replied coldly.

Two days later, my father called and asked both my sister and me to come over to the house at the same time. He wanted each of us to sign this "emotional peace treaty" so that we could be close again… the same way that he and his brother had been their whole lives. As we sat there in my father's den, he spoke in a very quiet tone. He barely had the strength to ask us to bury the hatchet, and to really be there for each other. He was afraid to leave this world without a resolution, as he would no longer be able to help us get past our past. He knew he was dying, and he wanted the war between us to end.

But in reality, there was no war. There was just me knocking on the door and begging to be let in, and my sister refusing to answer. For years, I tried my best to clear up my side of the street with her, as we had not talked since the incident at my grandmother's funeral, but she was like the quick-dry cement that my brother had used on my hand all those years ago. Only this time, no hammer in existence would break it. There was no compromise, no kindness, no generosity.

It was the fourth time I ever saw my father cry. The first time was when my parents got divorced, and the next two were at each of his parent's funerals. It was heartbreaking to witness. My father took responsibility for the lack-of-relationship my sister and I had with each other, and he felt like a failure. We both listened and vowed to try. It was all we could do.

The closer my father came to death, the more my brother and stepmother seemed to be in lock-step with their decisions, and it was very hard for me to break through the wall. Even though all of us shared in this profound sadness together, I still felt a bit like a stranger in my father's house. They would deal with their own feelings in a very non-verbal way, which was so foreign to me. My feelings have always been on my sleeve.

But I was not about to tell someone how they should or shouldn't grieve, so I simply worked hard to be of service in the best way I could, knowing that they were only going to let me in at a bare minimum.

I stole moments with my father whenever I could. On the Friday before he died, we spent some time together on his front patio as he sat in his wheelchair. I don't remember what we said to each other, but I remember the last thing he asked me to do.

"Would you light my cigarette?"

It was the one thing I would never have done in the last years of his life. My dad loved to smoke. He smoked anywhere, anytime, even though he tried so hard to quit. Once, when I went to his necktie factory to meet him for lunch, I was told that he was in the men's room, so that's where I went to let him know I was there.

I met him walking out of the bathroom… and he reeked of pot.

Pot? Really?!

I was stunned. "Dad, you don't smoke grass," I said.

"I know," he replied, "but I thought it would help me quit cigarettes."

Sadly, it didn't.

So I lit his cigarette for him. Without saying a word. Without uttering a sound. One last time, knowing in my heart that this was the end.

It was now Saturday, February 25, 2012. I had recently been cast in a little short film by a friend. On the way to rehearsal, I called my stepmother to let her know that I would be by around lunchtime, and I asked her if she needed anything.

"Yes," she said, "bring some paper towels."

Did she seriously just ask me for my help?

I was thrilled at the idea of getting to do anything to make life easier for my family. Just the idea of something as simple as picking up paper towels made me feel so useful, like I was part of the family... as odd as that sounds. I raced to the store before I got to work.

With the paper towels safely in my trunk, I walked into the rehearsal. Right as I was about to settle in, my cell phone rang. It was my brother. It was the call I had been dreading.

Our father had died.

I was out of my own body; I don't even remember what I said while walking out of the rehearsal. I drove to the house on autopilot. I walked in the front door and immediately hugged my stepmother; she seemed to be overwhelmed by my emotion. My sister was on her way, but as she was an Orthodox Jew and this was a Saturday, she was not allowed to drive from her home in the Fairfax area to our dad's home in the Hollywood Hills a few miles away.

So she walked. Seriously.

I couldn't shake my fog or make sense of anything. As we waited for the morgue to come and pick up his body, I remember asking the hospice worker, "Did you know he was going to pass this soon? I thought we had more time."

"We knew early this morning," she said.

Either from shock... or something else... my brother failed to tell me. It was the one thing I asked him to do for me, and he didn't do it. I didn't get the chance to be by my dad's side when he died, and it's something that still eats at me to this day. It was the most unwelcome feeling I think I've ever had. I felt like a foreigner in a strange country that didn't want me.

Later, I asked if I could do anything to help, aching to be involved in the planning of my father's funeral.

"Everything is taken care of," my family said. Even my uncle Mike, who had said that I could be there to help pick out the coffin, neglected to ask me to go with him when it happened. There was so much I was left out of.

The day before my father's funeral, the rabbi came to the house. As we sat around, he wanted to ask us questions about our father so that he could write a eulogy. He didn't know my dad at all, and I found the whole situation to be so odd. He took each of us one-by-one into the living room so we could share our stories with him.

On the day we would finally say goodbye, I was the only one who chose to speak at my dad's funeral. No one else wanted to, as they weren't used to speaking in public like I was. Of course, I had no idea that I would be sabotaged in my efforts. During the ceremony, the rabbi shared all of these stories about my dad that everyone had told him... including the ones that I was going to tell.

He stole my act! It was like an episode from a seventies sitcom.

Unbeknownst to me, my siblings sandbagged my speech by giving the rabbi all my material. I don't know if it was shock, grief, stress, or a combination of everything, but I found the entire moment to be hysterically funny. I now had no idea what I was going to say, but being in show business for my entire life, I had the ability to pull words out of thin air.

Hopefully! Oy!

I decided to go deep into my soul, so I told the most intimate stories of my father's late-night calls with me... his philosophies of life that he had been telling me since I was a baby boy. I told no one of these conversations, so no one but me even knew about them, and they just poured out of me.

My speech was surprisingly well-received as it came from my heart, and for one brief moment, much like Sally Field, I felt like they liked me… they really liked me! Once again, I used my art to get their approval as I had done so many times before in my life.

At the gravesite, the Jewish custom is to have your loved one lowered into the ground, and then have each family member take a shovel full of dirt and drop it over the coffin to help bury their deceased relative. After my mother took her turn, the rabbi helped her step back from the opening in the ground.

"Oh my God, you're so handsome," she whispered to him. "Are you single?"

"Ma!" I giggled… slightly surprised, slightly not.

"I'm just trying to get through this," she said. I had no idea that she would be as affected as she was by his passing. Apparently, they had kept in touch throughout the years after their divorce, and they still shared a sense of generosity with each other. After all, they had raised three children together. And deep down, I think he forgave her for her part in the demise of their marriage. And besides, both of them liked the attention.

The one who couldn't forgive her was my sister. That realization finally dawned on me after my father died. One afternoon, she came to my house to drop off photos and a DVD of my dad. Before I knew it, we had settled into a long conversation. We sat at my dining room table, and I remember so clearly the sheer anger that she still harbored toward our mother, whom she had not spoken to in many years. It seemed as if all the history had happened yesterday and not a lifetime ago. The hurt was born from Gloria's flamboyance and youthful indiscretions, and my sister was unable to handle the anguish they bestowed upon her.

We talked and we talked, and I remember her saying in a very solemn tone that she could see that I had changed, and how I was not the same person that I was in my twenties: a young kid making funny rude comments to get a rise out of her. I wasn't trying to get her attention anymore, or to get her to love me. I had created a life without her.

She looked at me and bowed her head. "If there's anything I ever did," she said, "then I'm sorry for that."

I had waited decades to hear this. Yet like the song from *A Chorus Line*, "I felt nothing." This woman who was sitting in front of me, so angry and hurt and in pain, was someone I didn't know. Too much time had passed; she was a stranger. I certainly had sympathy for what she felt, but the girl I went to the movies with, the girl who I ate corned beef sandwiches with, the girl who hung out with me at the comedy club, was not the girl who now sat at my dining room table with me.

I haven't seen her since. We've talked on the phone a couple of times, and while I wish things were different, it's just so hard for me to forgive someone who I feel has been so cruel to my mom. I don't know what's going to happen, for I've been wrong predicting the future before, but I know hope is best reserved for something to be hopeful about.

And I'm not there with her. Yet.

I did, however, catch a glimpse of hope with her daughter, N'Hamma, who now goes by the name Nicole. She was at my uncle Mike's funeral, and it was the first time I'd seen her since I'd met her briefly on that strange day at my father's house a week before his death. She's the youngest of my sister's four children. For years, unbeknownst to me, she had been rebelling against her strict Orthodox upbringing, and at seventeen decided to break from the faith from which she was raised. Many of my Jewish friends said that this was a common occurrence, considering how over-the-top the lifestyle is to some people.

Much to my sister and her husband's dismay, Nicole and I were in regular contact for a while, mainly through text and social media, though not as much lately. But there is hope that one day, I might be able to have a closeness with her that I have been unable to have with her mom.

Wow, that's nice to say!

Life is full of surprises. Isn't it something?

# 19

# The Birth of An Actor

My relationship with my father was forever complicated. He would usually wait until the end of the night before we could have a meaningful conversation. There was never a direct line on when he would connect with me. He would sit and eat Borscht with milk, and I would eat my favorite cereal with milk. To this day, I can't eat cereal without thinking about my dad. But I still don't like Borscht. It's awful.

When I moved out on my own, these late night conversations went from in-person to the phone. He would call me from his office in the house that he bought for my stepmother in the Hollywood Hills. She was usually sound asleep at the time. It was during these calls when he would share with me "his philosophy of life." It always seemed easier for him to talk on the phone than it was to speak face-to-face. And as time went on, the conversations went deeper.

I always took his advice to heart, even if I didn't always follow it the way he thought I should. When I told him that I wanted to be an actor, he said, "Vonderful, but I think you should be a psychiatrist… on the side."

Does playing one on a sitcom count?

My dad was a big believer in being prepared for anything life threw at you, and even more so when it came to the choices he made. He taught me to do the same. In my early acting days, before an audition, he would always tell me to show up and become indispensable.

I sat down one day to look back on the career I had cultivated. I realized that even after well over a hundred acting roles in film and television, I was still not getting opportunities to act in the kinds of projects I had dreamed about.

Maybe it was time to move to Palm Springs, buy a condo, and become the youngest guy on the block. Oy!

Over the years, the Hollywood system has changed a great deal. In the past, you could bank on the vast majority of roles being filmed in three places: Los Angeles, New York, or Canada, the latter where they won't let you work unless you're a star.

All that changed with the introduction of tax credits that individual states set up to lure prospective projects. New Mexico was an early adopter, landing major productions such as *Breaking Bad*. Other states followed suit, including North Carolina and Louisiana. I thought that casting a wider net might be a smart career move, so I got myself agents in each of the new burgeoning markets.

For two years, I applied for roles outside of LA by putting myself on video using my MacBook Air while sitting at my dining room table and using the accent wall.

Yes, I have an accent wall.

I landed a role in the Fox television series *Sleepy Hollow*, but it was nothing big enough to advance my career a great deal.

One day I got a call from my New Orleans agent, Brenda P. Netzberger, telling me that I had an audition for a movie filming in Georgia, which is possibly the biggest adopter of the tax credit system. It's gotten so big there that you can't flip through ten new shows without finding two or three that were shot there.

The director of the project needed video by noon the next day. Normally, this would not be terribly difficult, as I'd been putting together audition videos for dozens of projects that led nowhere. But this role was different. There were two scenes that took place in the 1800's, and one of them was a page-and-a-half monologue... all written with a dialect that I'd never done before.

If that wasn't bad enough, I had a stand-up gig that night, so I wouldn't even be able to work on it until the next morning... just a few hours before they needed it.

As I sat down to work, I thought to myself that I'm never, ever going to get this role. It never even occurred to me that it would be a possibility, but being my father's son, I did the work that was in front of me to the best of my ability.

I sent it off, and then I forgot about it.

A week later my agent called again to tell me I had a callback. The director of the project, this young guy named Nate Parker, wanted to meet me. Most of the time I didn't want to look up filmmakers I might work for because if it was somebody I really liked and respected, it would be very difficult to let go of the results of the audition. I would spend too much time thinking about it, a habit I still have yet to break.

To top it off, I had to fly to Savannah two days later on my own dime. If my time on the road gave me anything... it was frequent flier miles. With a few mouse clicks and a small dent in my stash of miles, I got on the plane.

My accommodations were not promising... to say the least. For two days, I stayed at this shit motel. When I got there, I saw a pregnant woman on her balcony... smoking a cigarette... while overlooking the pool that may or may not have been featured in *Leaving Las Vegas*. A man was laying out on something that resembled a beach chair. He looked like someone from the cast of *America's Most Wanted* (which I also guested on) who would kill me in my sleep.

I arrived at the audition three hours early. The audition wasn't even really in Savannah. It was a half hour away in a strip mall that you couldn't even find on a GPS. I pulled into this enormous parking lot and parked my rent-a-wreck. I then had lunch at this cute little southern restaurant that looked like an office that was decorated to look like a restaurant.

I went back to my car to rehearse my audition, which I had done the entire day before in my hotel room. The character was unsavory at best, who was a proponent of using the N-word in conversation as an adjective, a noun, and an interjection. I had never said that word out loud, except for singing along with Snoop Dogg in my car. With the windows up. And even then…

To be believable, I began to rehearse by saying it over and over again in my hotel room so I would not hesitate when I said it out loud in the audition. While rehearsing the N-word, there was a knock on my hotel room door. It was the housekeeper.

"What's going on in there?" she said.

Nothing… it's just a bunch of republicans talking. Kidding!

As I sat in my car at the strip mall going over my script, my father's words echoed somewhere in my subconscious mind. Make yourself indispensable.

As the minutes wound down to the audition, as I stood in front of my car acting out my part, a handsome man walked over to me and said, "I know you." It was Nate Parker – the writer, producer, director and star of the film for which I was auditioning. The film was the life story of black abolitionist Nat Turner, and it was called *The Birth of a Nation*.

I was taken aback, and I thought, 'Do I really have a fan in the middle of a strip mall parking lot a half hour outside of Savannah, Georgia?' He was so charming and confident, yet kind. I didn't quite hear what he said or how he said it, but it only took him a second to put me at ease. He had this innate power that made you feel like you were the only person in the room, and that it was safe to be yourself.

A few hours later, while reading for the part, he asked me to make an adjustment.

"The character is a bit more boisterous," he said. "Can you make him funnier?"

I thought to myself, 'Yeah, I've only been a stand-up comic as long as Donna Summer's been on the radio!'

"Yeah, I got this."

After the audition, Nate said, "Great job. Thank you for coming in."

"Good luck," I replied. "I think it's a wonderful project."

I walked out, thinking that it looked like a really important film… that I was never going to get. I drove to the airport and flew home.

The next day I got a call from my agent's assistant, Megan… this sweet southern gal with lots of kids… asking me how my day was going.

"It's fine," I said. "Why?"

"Because it's going to get a whole lot better," she replied. "You got the part!"

"That's great! What part?"

"Joseph Randall, the plantation owner in *The Birth of a Nation*!"

I instantly started to cry… totally forgetting that my friend Terry Ray was on the other line. This was the opportunity of a lifetime. I was going to make myself indispensable once again.

When the final draft of the script was ready, I worked every day with a different actor friend for seven days straight. I wanted to find the character, the nuance, the way he walked and talked. Joseph Randall was a plantation owner in 1831, after all. I wanted to get this right.

Then, I was off to Savannah… apprehensive, excited, and more importantly… ready. I had a feeling it was going to be a great experience; I just had no idea how much this would really mean to me, not just as an actor, but as a human being.

*The Birth of a Nation* is about Nat Turner, who was one of the first black men to fight back against white slave owners. His rebellion in 1831 was one of the origins of Black Lives Matter. The bravery of that particular man at that particular moment in time was extraordinarily powerful, and it moved me deeply.

To say that it was the most fulfilling project of my career would be an understatement. This was the kind of acting experience that you hear about on Bravo's *Inside the Actors Studio*. On the set, everyone knew that this film was as far from ordinary as it could possibly be. The story… the performances… the message… were simply on a different level. This was a film that could change people's views about racism in America, which, sadly, is still so desperately needed these days.

Most of my scenes were with Armie Hammer and Nate, but to call them merely scenes doesn't really do them justice. They were more like being a part of a theater company, and we were all in it together to create magic for a higher purpose. We weren't simply a bunch of actors and set professionals: we were a family with a mission.

And who knew that I – a liberal gay Jewish man in 2015 – would find that mission playing a racist heterosexual Christian plantation owner – in 1831? After decades of working on my craft, I was as far away from my true self as I could be, and I not only survived, but thrived in this challenge.

It's no mistake that a gifted black man, Nate Parker, gave this Jewish son of a Holocaust survivor and immigrant the opportunity to step up to the plate and hit it out of the park. And we would get to share this home run with the world at the Sundance Film Festival.

The night was January 25, 2016, and the crowd erupted in thunderous applause. They had just seen what many have called a transformative and important piece of filmmaking. Nate Parker was on the stage for a cast Q & A after the show, but the stars of the film were not enough for him. This was his newly adopted family, after all, so he then invited literally every member of the production who was in attendance up to the stage to share in this with each other. The moderator joked that this might just be the largest cast and crew Q & A in the history of Sundance.

Thom Senzee wrote a cover story piece on me called "The Birth of an Actor" for *Rage Monthly*… a local magazine in San Diego. He asked if he could get a quote from Nate.

I said, "The film opens in a week; I really don't think he's going to have time to write something, but you can call his publicist. It couldn't hurt to ask."

Surprisingly, and unsurprisingly, Nate did take the time to write something.

"It was really all about his incredible work in the audition room," replied Parker. "I wanted to stray away from the traditional sociopathic slave owner, and instead present a character who had more relatable qualities – qualities some could almost perceive as 'likeable.' This would create in an audience member a more complex journey as they grappled with the systemic effects of this period of American history. Jason walked in with an understanding of this vision. He brought a confidence, humility, and humor to the role in a way that helped achieve a much needed balance across the characters, and overall narrative. His on-set instincts further validated his hiring, as he constantly pursued brave choices that aided in expanding the breadth of his character."[1]

When I read that, I never felt so "heard" and "seen" in my career. Friends, industry associates, and fans reacted with an incredible amount of goodwill towards me, in appreciation for me as an out gay actor being able to not only play the role convincingly, but the fact that I got the role at all. It was incredibly meaningful to me.

Reliving that moment on that stage at Sundance makes me realize that acting truly is the love of my life, and the deeper the project, the deeper that love feels. As I left the theatre that night, I remember thinking to myself that this was it: through this film, people were going to see a side of me that they may never have known existed. New, important, challenging roles would fly through my door. My life as an actor would be forever changed, and I had my experience in *The Birth of a Nation* to thank for it.

And then, the bottom fell out.

An opinion piece came out in *The New York Times* by Roxane Gay. She wrote about how there was renewed interest in Nate Parker and his

---

[1] Quote from "The Birth of an Actor" in *Rage Weekly*, reprinted with permission by Thom Senzee.

history of sexual assault. She said that she was not able to separate the artist from his art.

In 1999, Nate Parker was charged with rape at Penn State University. The charges were brought by a woman with whom he already had a consensual sexual relationship, who accused him of raping her while she was intoxicated.

A year and a half later, Nate was acquitted of the charges.

Thirteen years after the night in question, she committed suicide, leaving behind a child.

*The New York Times* article was especially damaging because it was the personal point of view of a woman who said that she had her own experience with sexual violence, and as such could not be impartial, even though she tries.

She went on to say that her gut instinct leads her to believe the victim in such cases since the only thing to be gained by going public is potential humiliation and scorn from the public.

Let me make this perfectly clear: I have the utmost respect and support for the right of any woman to say no at any time. I would fight for any woman who is raped or sexually assaulted. There is never, ever any excuse for it to happen.

The reality is that there are countless cases in almost every college or university each week of kids being stupid, getting drunk, and having sex before consent is either given or denied. And if there is a history of consensual sexuality between the two parties, consent is the expected reaction.

Today is the dawn of a new age of consent, and in this age of consent, hopefully, we'll be free to talk on a deeper level and the blurred line will become clear.

The fallout was that this brilliant film that had won the top two prizes at Sundance… the Best Film and Best Audience Awards… a film that had gotten a standing ovation at each of the two screenings at the Toronto

International Film Festival… and reviews that had seemed to be written by all our mothers… would forever have a cloud hanging over it.

The Academy Awards, the Golden Globe Awards, and the Screen Actors Guild Awards shunned it, though Nate was nominated for the Outstanding Directorial Achievement in a First Time Feature Film by the Directors Guild of America.

Nevertheless, the film did become an award winner, with a total of twenty-six nominations and four wins. With a box office take of almost sixteen million dollars, the film was a bigger success than many people were willing to acknowledge. But the sadness was that because of what happened at Penn State University in 1999, a message that the world so desperately needed was received by a smaller audience than had been hoped for.

But for me, I'm forever changed for having the opportunity to show up and be my best self. No matter what is said, my work is there for all to see, and it has led me on a path to the next chapter of my work as an artist.

Growing up, my dad always told me that when I go to an audition, wear a tie. I took that to mean 'show up and be your best self.'

Thank you, Dad. I'm still wearing your ties.

# Epilogue

## I'm Not Dead Yet!

Well, I didn't get the husband, and I didn't get the great follow-up role (in a studio) film after *The Birth of a Nation*, but I haven't stopped working since. But I did get a great role in the romantic dram called *Hank* and a very J.K. Simmons ish role as a private investigator in *Immortal*. But sometimes you move up ten steps, then you have to go back five. But as Elaine Stritch said in Stephen Sondheim's *Company*, "I'm still heeeeeere!"

I'm often asked if I would have pursued this career had I known what was going to happen, and my pat answer is always, "No way." And the reason is much like Albert Brooks in *Defending Your Life*: there would be too many parts that would scare the shit out of me. I'm too much of an emotional wuss to deal with all that pain.

I walked into this career thinking that I was the one who everyone wanted… that they were somehow waiting for me, and that God had chosen me. But then I realized that this was not how the universe always works. But I was stubborn, I was tenacious, and I was sure that this is where I should be. And along the way, I fell in love with the craft of being an actor and comedian.

I read somewhere that a good friend of Barbra Streisand's had a niece, and asked Barbra if she would meet with her. Barbra said yes. When they met, the girl asked, "Do you think I should be an actress?"

"No," said Barbra.

"Why?"

"Because if you have to ask, then you don't really want it."

I would take her words a step further. For me, acting is not just a want, it's a need… as important to me as eating, breathing, or sleeping. It's like a lover that you can't get out of your heart.

In 2018, I fell in love with a man named Antonio who once said to me, "I miss feeling your breath on my neck." He was Italian, and what I would call a new gay, as he only came out about ten years prior. He was like a collectible figurine: still in the box, unblemished by human hands. Like an unopened *Star Wars* figure, he had that new gay-car smell.

He married a man who he thought he loved, so that he could come to America to be, what he called, free. He came from a small town in Sicily that would not be considered a safe place to come out. His parents even told him that they hated gay people, not knowing that he was gay. As far as I know, he has yet to tell them, which makes me so sad that I skip a breath.

For months he told me that it was over between him and his husband, and that when the time was right, if I would just hold out a little bit longer, that we could be together. Only, a little bit longer never seemed to end. And then one day he told me that he was still in love with his husband. And then when he told me that he still loved me too, I replied as Harvey Fierstein did in the play *Torch Song Trilogy*: "Just not enough." And then I broke it off.

He apologized profusely and told me that he hated himself for it, but he had to try to make it work with his husband. I felt like I had been pushed off the edge of a cliff that had no bottom in sight.

And now you're thinking, 'Is this the way he's going to end his book?'

And my answer is, "No."

Every morning when I wake up, I create a gratitude list of everything I have. My mom is alive and kicking; we make fun of each other and laugh all the time. I have a great apartment and a car that runs. Yeah, it's a Prius, but it gets fourteen thousand miles to the gallon. I have the best friends in the world who I can call, who will be at my side at a moment's notice. And

I have a career which I've gotten to work with some of the most talented people in show business, and the possibility of more to come.

No, I haven't found the love of my life, and I'm always waiting for that next role which feeds me as an artist (that people will actually get to see), but what I do know is that I'm standing where my feet are.

And most days, I'm pretty good with that.

# About the Authors

When you think of one of the most prolific character actors, who's also an outrageously openly gay stand-up comedian, one name comes to mind: Jason Stuart. He has a major role in *The Birth of a Nation* by filmmaker Nate Parker. Jason has also appeared in the award winning films *Hank, Immortal, Tangerine, Love is Strange, Gia*, with *Kindergarten Cop* and *Vegas Vacation* among his fan favorites. He has wowed TV audiences with guest roles on such shows as *Swedish Dicks, Love, Sleepy Hollow, Real Rob, Entourage, The Closer, It's Always Sunny in Philadelphia, House, Everybody Hates Chris, George Lopez, Will & Grace, Charmed*, and as the wildly popular "Dr. Thomas" on *My Wife & Kids*. As a stand-up comic, you have laughed with him on *Gotham Comedy Life, Red Eye with Tom Shillue, One Night Stand Up, Wisecrack, Comics Unleashed with Byron Allen, Out There In Hollywood* and his own comedy special *Making It to the Middle*. He currently resides in California… alone again.

Dan Duffy has been working in film, television, and radio for over twenty-five years. In 2002, Dan was diagnosed with stage-three testicular cancer. He wanted to change the way people looked at a cancer diagnosis, so he has blogged extensively for *Huffington Post* and *Medium*, and wrote *The Half Book: He's Taking His Ball and Going Home*. Dan has shared his message throughout the country, including speaking at Stanford Medicine X in 2016 and 2017, keynoting at the American Cancer Society Cancer Action Network Conference, and speaking at TEDxSarasota in 2013. Dan and his wife Stephanie have been married since 2003, and they have two sons, Sam and Ben.